"If you want to make your life a masterpiece, then read *The Deeper Path*. Kary provides the tools you need to tap into your talents and desires and live your true potential."

Mark Sanborn, *New York Times*, *Wall Street Journal*, and *BusinessWeek* bestselling author of *The Fred Factor*

"Kary invites us to take off the mask we hide behind and reveal our true selves. Once removed, we find we aren't alone. With practical insights and actionable steps, *The Deeper Path* gently moves us out of our comfort zones and into a place of love and healing. Once there, we discover our ultimate purpose."

Jason Locy, author of *Veneer*

"Though we may wish it weren't so, life is messy and filled with pain. In *The Deeper Path*, Kary Oberbrunner reveals that what we believe are inevitable burdens may actually be unexpected gifts. With humility and wisdom far exceeding his years, Kary lights the way forward to a healed life of purpose and joy."

Jonathan Merritt, author of *A Faith of Our Own*

"A compelling model of transformation. Kary's examples from all sectors of society make this a dynamic read for the faith and business communities alike."

Harvey Hook, author of *The Power of an Ordinary Life* and executive director of The Gathering

"Many people have an intellectual understanding of the principles found in this book; few can express them in words and action, and that is what Kary has done and who he is. Don't read this book, study it!"

Paul Martinelli, internationally acclaimed speaker, trainer, and coach

"*The Deeper Path* teaches us that numbing our pain is numbing our potential. Kary's words challenge us to consider a new way of thinking and then equip us to take that journey ourselves."

Scott M. Fay, internatio

D1328665

Also by Kary Oberbrunner

Your Secret Name

The Fine Line

Called

The Journey Towards Relevance

THE DEEPER PATH

Five Steps That Let Your Hurts Lead to Your Healing

KARY OBERBRUNNER

BakerBooks

a division of Baker Publishing Group
Grand Rapids, Michigan

Published by Baker Books
a division of Baker Publishing Group
P.O. Box 6287, Grand Rapids, MI 49516-6287
www.bakerbooks.com

Printed in the United States of America

Library of Congress Cataloging-in-Publication Data
Oberbrunner, Kary, 1976–
    The deeper path : five steps that let your hurts lead to your healing / Kary
Oberbrunner.
      p.   cm.
    ISBN 978-0-8010-1521-2 (pbk.)
    1. Suffering—Religious aspects—Christianity. I. Title.
    BV4909.O24 2013
    248.8′6—dc23   2012035433

The internet addresses, email addresses, and phone numbers in this book are accurate at the time of publication. They are provided as a resource. Baker Publishing Group does not endorse them or vouch for their content or permanence.

Published in association with Creative Trust Literary Group, 5141 Virginia Way, Suite 320, Brentwood, TN 37027

13   14   15   16   17   18   19   7   6   5   4   3   2   1

For my parents,
Mike and Linda Oberbrunner,
who gave me life.

And for my "builder,"
Chet Scott,
who helped me discover my
"Why."

Pain is inevitable. Misery is a choice.

Unknown

Contents

Beneath the Surface   9

The Deeper Path   11

Part 1   Numb—The Why

1 A Routine Takeoff   17

2 The Melody Line   23

3 The Door of Pain   33

4 Leaving the Nursery   41

5 The Little Difference   59

Part 2   Feel—The How

6 Step One: Question Your Condition   77

7 Step Two: Unmask Your Painkillers   85

8 Step Three: Explore Your Wounds   99

9 Step Four: Overcome Your Excuses   109

10 Step Five: Embody Your Healing   119

Part 3 Alive—The What

11 One Happy Reunion   131

12 God of Edges   141

13 Soul on Fire   151

14 Author Your OPUS   157

15 Five-Minute Sketch   181

Discussion Points   185

Examples of OPUS   189

Acknowledgments   195

Notes   197

Beneath the Surface

There are two days of your life that stand out, far above the rest:

> The day you were born
> and
> The day you discovered why

This book is written for those who desire an answer to the "why" question, and this answer is found only by taking The Deeper Path.

The Deeper Path

Those who turn back, remember the ordeal. Those who persevere, remember the adventure.

Milo Arnold

I'm writing this book with one hand—my left one. Nothing against the left-handed population; I respect and care for those folks too. But I'm right-handed and I've written all my books with both hands.

Except this one.

Seventeen years ago something happened to me, and I felt only ignorance at the time. The doctors finally caught it three months ago, so I recently had surgery. I never had surgery before, but now I'm no longer a surgery virgin. I can stand at the water cooler and swap stories about being "put under."

Except where I work we don't have a water cooler. And I don't really drink much water anyway, though I know I should. At least that's what the experts tell us. Besides, I don't even use the term *water cooler*.

But back to seventeen years ago: I was in wrestling practice and did a move called a standing switch. Only I did the move incorrectly and my right shoulder paid the price. And although I didn't hear a tear, I felt one.

I remember yelling. It was a Deep, genuine, from-the-belly yell. I hate those yells. They usually accompany a long recovery with some internal excavation and a bit of soul surgery.

I really don't like the word *surgery*, which is why for seventeen years I ignored the Pain in my shoulder. Avoidance usually worked. But in the back of my mind, I knew something was wrong. Once in a while, when things got too Painful, I numbed the Pain with some over-the-counter meds, especially when playing sports.

Some might not call it a sport, but I do enjoy an occasional round of disc golf. It's a fun, low-cost, high-reward activity.

Looking back, my game always felt a little off. Certain throws produced a dull Pain. I even stayed away from a few types of throws altogether (like the tomahawk and side arm) because they made my Pain worse. The friends I play disc golf with never knew about my Pain, since I masked it well. I don't like people who make excuses, so I simply ignored the Pain and those particular throws for seventeen years.

But three months ago, all that changed.

Around Thanksgiving, my six-year-old son, Keegan; my brother-in-law, Mike; my father-in-law; and I were all out in wintry Michigan playing disc golf. We came to a little creek with a large pipe that spanned the ten-foot-wide stream of water.

Although there was a bridge for easy crossing, my adventurous Keegan had a different idea. (We can't be too hard on him, because his name means "little fiery one.") Rather excitedly, he asked if he could walk across on the pipe. I tossed some encouragement his way, and instantaneously he shot up in proper posture. Given the cold weather, I decided to join him as he crossed to the other side, in case he hadn't quite mastered his balance yet.

He insisted he had learned this skill from Sensei Wu, the star of his favorite cartoon, *Lego Ninjago*. But his mother's warnings rang loud in my subconscious, so I assumed a supporting stance.

He made it halfway across and then started to teeter. Seeing his instability, my reflexes kicked in and I lunged for his listing body, now only two feet from the cold water. My right arm snatched him just in time. Given his light weight, I managed to pull him awkwardly back onto the pipe.

We giggled, finished crossing, and generously doled out a round of high fives to his grandpa and uncle, witnesses to his bravery and our close call. If only we had walked away with just memories pumping through our brains and adrenaline pumping through our veins. Instead, I also carried with me a second tear in my shoulder. A week later, when I could no longer lift my arm, I knew I couldn't avoid the truth or the Pain any longer.

I needed to see a specialist and I knew my choice probably brought a cost with it, but I had no idea how much.

This Deeper Path demanded an MRI, a surplus of medical bills, three months of physical therapy, lost days of work, a deadline extension, extra time when flying in a plane, the need to ask people for help, and hardest of all for me, a ban from wrestling with my kids.

I did, however, learn a lot through the process. For starters, I discovered an unknown fear of mine. The MRI experience produced a severe claustrophobic reaction. I bet I looked odd kissing the ground after the technician pulled me out of the machine that day.

But I also learned that overcoming chronic Pain—like a torn labrum—sometimes requires experiencing new kinds of Pain—like surgery. I learned that sometimes our hurt is the only thing that leads us into our healing. Quite honestly, if I hadn't received that second tear three months ago, I'd still be walking around ignorant of the initial tear from seventeen years ago.

Although I'm presently in Pain and still healing, the truth is I no longer have two tears in my labrum. The surgeon repaired both and officially pronounced my shoulder healed.

Best of all, I'm told my disc golf game will be better than ever. And if all goes according to plan, I'm sure in a few short months I'll wonder why I waited so long.

〰〰〰〰

Like me, you have Pain in your life. But for most of us, this Pain may go unnoticed—for years.

We ignore the Pain. We mask it. We numb it. We get used to the limitations our Pain brings, and we simply adjust. We manage, settle, cope. We live way below our abilities simply because we're unwilling to pursue the Pain that would push us to reach our potential. We hide our hurts and, in the process, we sabotage our healing.

But this doesn't have to be true. If we're willing—and brave—we can choose The Deeper Path.

And this Deeper Path makes all the difference.

Before we celebrate this secret, we should first examine its price tag. Going beneath the surface comes with a cost, and the general population prefers to stay at ground level for a reason.

Anyone who engages in even the smallest form of excavation will agree that we need the right kind of equipment. Randomly slamming our shovels into the earth won't get us very far. In order to be strategic, we'll get properly equipped before we begin excavating. We'll examine the why, the how, and the what of The Deeper Path.[1]

Prepare to get a little dirty: going five steps down tends to have that effect. But also expect some adventure too. Along the way, we'll meet a few brave souls—and a few crazy ones.

Anyone who's taken The Deeper Path, and returned to speak about it, will say it's worth it. But not all return. If they did, more of us might follow their example.

My ultimate purpose in writing this book—left-handed, mind you—is that you become one of these few. You're too important not to be included in this elite class.

Ironically, in order to take The Deeper Path, we'll start by examining a specific takeoff. It might sound a little strange—go up to go down? Then again, the world we're about to explore might feel a little strange at first.

Even though the flight might be a little bumpy, I know you'll love where we land.

PART 1

NUMB

The Why

1

A Routine Takeoff

I run on the road, long before I dance under the lights.

Muhammad Ali

On January 15, 2009, the sun rose like on any other day, and 155 people awoke, packed their bags, said their good-byes, and headed to the airport expecting nothing unusual—like most of us do, on most of our days.

Lucky for them, they buckled in for the flight of their lives. Even luckier for them, their particular pilot would soon be touted as a hero on the evening news.

Everything started out rather predictably—the spiel from the flight attendants about wearing the oxygen masks in the case of an emergency, the reminder to fasten their safety belts, the semi-awkward attempt to greet the stranger in the adjacent seat. Minutes later the plane raced down the runway and became airborne, along with musings about the day that now lay spread out for the seizing.

Like clockwork, the clock worked the way it should, bringing routine right along with it. Fortunately, this particular routine proved to be exceptionally routine, creating potential space for reading, writing, and even dozing for a few sleepy souls.

But only ninety seconds into the flight, the pilot noticed an unexpected obstacle. Or more accurately, unexpected *obstacles*. Birds suddenly filled his view.

Lots of birds. Lots of *big* birds.

In his book *Highest Duty*, Captain Chesley "Sully" Sullenberger explains that the Canada geese with six-foot wingspans, weighing eight to eighteen pounds each, sounded like large hail pelting the plane. Moments later he felt what every pilot fears—double engine failure resulting from a brutal bird strike.[1]

Routine had suddenly been blown to pieces—along with the birds.

The plane lost thrust and, given its low speed and low altitude over New York City, one of the most densely populated areas on the planet, Captain Sully knew he sat front and center in a seriously challenging situation.

Despite the fact that he had never requested this experience, in that instant, life sought his response. And 154 people prayed that Captain Sully's response would prove to be the right one.

⊥⊥⊥⊥⊥

We all have at least one defining moment in our lifetime. Many of us have a handful more. We can't predict them. And we can't create them—at least not easily.

But defining moments are coming for us. They will hunt us down and find us. They're not for us or against us. They simply are. They're a mirror, a complex combination of circumstances, impressions, tones, shades, vibrations, and events meant to do one solitary thing: reveal us. What's inside of us is going to come out. And whether we welcome our response or whether we'd like to reverse time and bury our response right back where it came from, know this: the world is watching.

We were going to see Captain Sully on the evening news that January day. Regardless of the pilot's actions following the unlucky bird strike, his number had come up, and life had decided to snatch him from semi-anonymity and thrust him onto center stage.

Through a series of events he couldn't avoid, Captain Sully faced his defining moment. And he faced it without the:

Privilege of cultivating an optimistic attitude
Possibility of guaranteeing a good marriage
Ability of phoning a friend or being a friend
Opportunity of consulting his pilot's manual
Chance of contemplating best practices
Convenience of researching solutions
Benefit of a cost analysis projection
Time to formulate a strategic plan
Option of creating a healthy body
Luxury of ensuring a sharp mind
Chance to settle with the Creator

Nope. Life happened and he didn't have time for anything except an immediate response. But this is precisely what made Captain Sully a hero. And he didn't need a bird strike to tell him that. He already knew the secret that sets people like him apart. He acknowledged the reality that is no respecter of persons, race, age, intelligence, income, or education. He knew The Deeper Path and, more importantly, he traveled The Deeper Path.

Unfortunately, although this truth is available to all, it's understood by only a few. And despite this truth lurking in the shadows on most days, every so often, like on January 15, 2009, life decides to invite it into our awareness, even if for only a brief moment.

But what if we could tease this truth out of hiding, study it, and employ it to our advantage? What if we could make it work for us and not against us? That wouldn't be fair, now, would it?

Like me, you've probably been sold the same claustrophobic cliché your entire life—that life isn't fair. Well, what if in this situation it is? What if the universe operates according to specific laws and Sully simply used them to his advantage?

Here's what I mean: most people accept the Law of Gravity. For example, despite our best intentions, if we step off a cliff, we're going to fall and crash at the bottom. This law is no respecter of persons—unless we have a hang glider, jet pack, parachute, or some other invention strapped to our back. Unless we bend the law by knowing the law and by putting it to work for us. Unless we "cheat the system."

So what if we could cheat the system with other laws too? What if this is what Captain Sully did?

Imagine the possibilities.

We could shortcut heartaches, ensure successes, and take strides ahead of our competition. We could excel in relationships, avoid emotional blowups, and center ourselves before uncertainty comes knocking.

We could choose our response ahead of time and guarantee that our defining moments would define us exactly the way we desired.

Many people want none of it. To admit The Deeper Path exists is to admit the need to interact with it. Therefore, many dismiss January 15, 2009, as a fluke or an example of luck in its purest form. Many prefer to label the whole experience as a miracle. And that's just what they did, referring to this event as the "Miracle on the Hudson."[2]

But it wasn't a miracle. For the record, I do believe in miracles. I've read about them and have even experienced a few, but I also believe in The Deeper Path that Captain Sully knew and understood. Fortunately for his passengers, he didn't just know this Path; he practiced it and put it to work for him. In the process he achieved "the most successful ditching in aviation history."[3]

Was he a hero?

You bet, and the rest of the crew with him. They rightfully received the highest award in aviation. But this "miracle" wasn't simply happenstance. Rather, this successful emergency landing on the Hudson River resulted from a series of decisions determined long before, and birthed out of something much Deeper.

As Captain Sully told CBS news anchor Katie Couric, "For 42 years, I've been making small, regular deposits in this bank of experience: education and training. And on January 15 the balance was sufficient so that I could make a very large withdrawal."[4]

Know this: your number will come up. I can't tell you the exact day of your defining moment, but trust me, it's coming. And it doesn't care if you're ready.

Now our friends and family, they do care. They're rooting for our success and want us to land safely. But let's be honest: they have a vested interest too. None of us is flying alone. We all have passengers with us. They're belted in behind us, praying that our response will prove to be the right one.

But this is much bigger than even the "passengers" directly connected to us. Consider that US Airways Flight 1549 landed in the Hudson River adjacent to midtown Manhattan. Thousands of innocent New Yorkers were engaged in their normal routines that day, completely oblivious to the mass of metal with full fuel tanks descending directly on top of them. You get the picture.

Both our action *and* our inaction directly *and* indirectly affect our world.

The choice is ours: Do we want to shake the dice and wait until our unexpected bird strike before we determine our response? If Captain Sully had waited, he, the crew, the passengers, and the plane would have gone down in flames like other flights before his.[5]

The world is waiting on you to get past what you're waiting for. We need you to convert your apprehension into productive energy. We need you to dig Deep and act *today*. We need you to take The Deeper Path. Tomorrow could be your defining moment, the day when your number is drawn.

Use today to prepare for tomorrow.

Know that we're behind you.

And we want you to land safely.

Because we have a vested interest.

2

The Melody Line

It's a beautiful day, don't let it get away.

U2

Whether or not you're a fan of the Dublin-based rock band U2, if you've heard their song "Beautiful Day" on your iPod or over the airwaves, you might automatically recall the melody line. For others, maybe we needed the sticky nine words above to conjure up the melody line, and now we're in another world, singing the entire song.

Melody lines wield that type of power and that type of potential.

As we might expect, Bono, humanitarian and main vocalist of U2, is often associated with the term *melody line*. He's a singer, after all, and for one of the biggest rock bands of all time.

But what might surprise you is how Bono himself uses that term.

If you're a nonmusical person like me: the technical meaning of *melody line* refers to "a linear succession of musical tones perceived as a single entity. In its most literal sense, a melody is a combination of pitch and rhythm."[1]

Still in the dark?

Don't worry.

23

Me too.

I'm the guy who used to butcher the song "Happy Birthday" at staff get-togethers. People pay me *not* to sing. I don't know what a melody line is and I certainly can't sing one either. My colleagues will back me on this point.

No worries.

Bono's alternative definition of the melody line emerged around the same time he cofounded ONE, a grassroots advocacy and campaigning organization. ONE fights extreme poverty and preventable disease, particularly in Africa, by raising public awareness and pressuring political leaders to support smart and effective policies and programs that are saving lives, helping to put kids in school, and improving futures.[2]

ONE boasts of a big vision, but the literally billion-dollar question begs, "How does someone make that vision stick?" David Lane, ONE's chief executive officer and former executive director of the Bill and Melinda Gates Foundation, labored closely with Bono in order to do just that.

Lucky for us, authors Jeffery Cohn and Jay Moran shed a little sunshine on the situation in their book *Why Are We Bad at Picking Good Leaders?*

> Bono and Lane constantly honed their message or what they referred to as "the melody line." In musical terms a melody line is simply a line of rising or falling notes that gives a song its recognizable theme. It's part of the song that a listener remembers, the notes that stand out above the rest. Bono and Lane turned this into a metaphor for giving voice to their organization's big ideas. The melody line was how they communicated their vision to the masses to inspire and unite them. The key was to make sure that the melody line connected with people and tapped into their Deepest values and aspirations.[3]

Simply put, an effective melody line:

Connects with people and taps into their Deepest values and
    aspirations
Is the part of the song the listener *remembers*
Gives *voice* to the big idea

Unpacking these concepts helps us understand the true significance of a well-defined melody line.

How Well Do You Connect?

Before our message can connect with others, it must first connect with us. No one will hear our melody line if they don't believe us. Every message flows out of a messenger, so if the messenger lacks credibility, then it's difficult to extend credibility to the message.

Sincerity connects because it's so rare. We find ourselves in the age of ad saturation; according to experts we're exposed to over three thousand ads a day, and so we can quickly tell if we're being sold something.[4]

Our antenna is up and our tolerance is down.

Every person asks three questions when they hear a messenger for the first time. I call them the connection questions:

1. Do you care for me?
2. Can I trust you?
3. Can you help me?

If the answers are yes, then the messenger and the message tend to stick much better.

The more we understand who we are and all the little nuances associated with that, the better chance we have at knowing our song, singing our song well, and connecting the melody line of that song with our listeners.

How Will You Be Remembered?

Bestselling author John Maxwell says, "People will summarize your life in one sentence, pick it now."[5]

Although we can't control what people think of us, we can control the way we present ourselves, including our attitudes. We're each emitting a frequency, and it's our choice whether it's positive or negative.

Our frequency projects much further than we imagine. According to the Law of Transmutation, the dominating frequency of what we think and believe will transmute into what our results are. We possess much more control than we realize.

If our frequency feels lethargic, passive, and uninspiring, then our results will be likewise. We will benefit by realizing that we can't outdo our attitude or outperform our self-image. Similarly, who we are is what we attract. We shouldn't feel threatened by this reality because this law isn't set against us. It simply is.

What's Your Big Idea?

Our frequency matters, but so does our message. And although the feel of our melody line evokes emotion, the lyrics associated with our melody line linger long after the music ends.

Words carry weight because they inspire ideas. And ideas can change the world. We observe this in Leonardo DiCaprio's character Cobb from the film *Inception*. Although a fictional story, this commentary on the power of an idea is also couched in truth.

Cobb explains, "What's the most resilient parasite? An idea. A single idea from the human mind can build cities. An idea can transform the world and rewrite all the rules."[6]

Our melody line matters because it's the voice to our big idea.

A message without a voice is simply a thought and a message with too many voices is simply a noise.

Regrettably, we'll soon discover that a noise never sticks.

Since we find ourselves at the beginning of this book, I thought it would serve us both if I took a moment to define its "melody line."

First, what it's not:

It's not about Captain Sully or Bono or the ONE campaign.

It's not about education, entertainment, or distraction.

It's not about landing a job or landing a plane.

On the contrary, this book is specifically about *you*.

It's written because I care about you and your transformation. I care about your melody line, maybe even more than you do at this point. (I know: a tough truth to try on, right? But hang with me a little and I'll prove it.)

Those who know you like you just the way you are, but they like you too much to leave you that way.

We need you to reach higher than you've ever imagined and to do so you must dig Deeper than you ever have before.

I'm committed to helping you by leveraging all I can, borrowing examples from every segment of society, and drawing upon those who have gone before. I'm willing to jump in at times with my own story of Pain if it has a chance of helping you understand yours.

I'm giving you my best because I believe you're worth it. I believe you're created in the image of God himself, equipped and endowed with a distinct personality, skillset, and destiny.

On the day you were conceived, the Designer took your unique genetic code and said, "You are amazing. I'll never let the world experience my masterpiece in this way ever again."

Understand that you possess unique characteristics, emotions, and desires. Similar to sports teams retiring jersey numbers as a way to honor key contributors, including players and coaches, the Creator "retires" your (genetic) number forever. And just as sports teams usually display these numbers by hanging banners from the rafters of their home arena, God desires to proudly display you in his home forever.

I wouldn't be surprised if you didn't believe me. Many times we're brainwashed into believing we're nothing more than lumps of flesh infused with electrical impulses, random accidents who arrived on the scene—replaceable, dispensable, cheap.

I beg to differ.

I trust God when he calls you his workmanship (see Eph. 2:10). The Greek word is *poiema*, meaning, "a work of God." Perhaps you even recognize that word; it's the same root as our English word *poem*.

Hear that? You're God's poem.

A mistake? Not a chance.

Worthless? Try again.

I cart worthless things to my curb once a week, and I've never camped out at my curb protecting my garbage. Go ahead, feel free to steal it. I wouldn't miss seeing or *smelling* my garbage ever again. And I'm sure you feel the same about yours.

We leave worthless things unguarded because they're . . . worthless. But when it comes to life, why do you leave yourself unprotected?

Why are there areas of your heart and soul that are parked on the curb of life, available for anyone to steal?

Contrast that with something irreplaceable like time. For me, I guard my time fiercely. I say no to all kinds of opportunities so that I can say yes to what really matters. I never want to reach the end of my life and say with regret, "I wish I would have invested more time in the Deeper things of life."

This wasn't always the case. Before I knew The Deeper Path, I didn't value my time. I held my time carelessly because I wasn't doing anything great or becoming anything great.

Randomly coasting through life, I embodied *unintentional*. I failed to build anything, including myself.

Think about how we describe spending unintentional time: we "waste time" or "kill time."

Author M. Scott Peck insightfully writes, "Until you value yourself, you won't value your time."[7] He thinks that wasting time indicates a much Deeper issue, one that cannot be remedied without some deliberate digging.

Are you beginning to hear the music? Your soul is worth something. And the way you see yourself greatly influences the way you see the world.

Although this might be our song, it's still not our melody line.

Thankfully, you're curious enough to excavate further, and restless enough to dig Deeper. This sets you apart. You're divinely discontent—not in an ungrateful kind of way, but in an explorative one. You're not pacified with clichés or simple explanations.

No. You want the truth. No matter how difficult it is.

Although I congratulate you for wanting to know, simply knowing is not enough. You have to see it for yourself. This book is that vision: an expedition into hearing the melody line and seeing it too.

But before we dig too Deep, first, a little something about our trip: Pain is inevitable.

I always appreciate doctors or dentists who give me a heads-up. The phrase, "This is going to sting a little," went a long way in building trust, even when I was a kid. The professional who simply stuck me without warning failed to earn my trust. Quite honestly, I ended up resenting them, even if their motivation was to protect me from the truth.

Tell me the ouch is coming, because I can handle it if I know it's coming.

In an attempt to earn your trust, take this as my advance warning: if you keep reading Pain will appear in your immediate future. It has to. Our path can't be Pain-free because life isn't. And although we know this, we've been led to believe life should be Pain-free.

We take great measures to insulate and isolate ourselves from Pain. This is our model from infancy. I remember driving each one of our newborn babies home from the hospital. Though they were buckled into a protective car seat and surrounded by four walls of airbags, twenty mph still felt too fast to me. My wife, Kelly, and I cushioned their reality, pushing Pain out the door.

But given enough time, Pain eventually breaks through and corners us. When it does, most of us run for cover. We numb ourselves, because when we're numb we don't feel anything—the good or the bad. We shout for our savior, noise, to come rescue us and drown out our ache. We busy ourselves by asking activity to join us.

Unfortunately, by fleeing our Pain we inadvertently also flee our potential.

Life gives us plenty of escape buttons to press when we feel our Pain mounting. These distractions and diversions serve as coping strategies and survival tactics. Seventeenth-century French philosopher Blaise Pascal observed them and accurately forewarned us of their lethal effects:

> The only thing that consoles us for our miseries is distraction, yet that is the greatest of our wretchednesses. Because that is what mainly prevents us from thinking about ourselves and leads us imperceptibly to damnation. Without it we should be bored, and boredom would force us to search for a firmer way out, but distraction entertains us and leads us imperceptibly to death.[8]

Pascal believed that boredom would eventually lead to our escape. Yet he also believed that anesthetizing our pain unconsciously invites mediocrity. And no one can argue that we are a world of mediocrity.

I wonder what Pascal would think of our distractions today. Spending endless hours plugged into video games, excavating Facebook statuses, and consuming reality TV leaves us numb and unfulfilled. Vicariously living through someone else's life always leaves us wanting more.

We're spirit, not just flesh. We're meant to show up present in our own lives. We're meant to be fully alive, not half dead. We're designed for a fuller expression and fuller expansion of what we currently experience. We long for more—more resources to share, more compassion to give, more fulfillment to experience, more purpose to taste, more peace to feel, and more joy to spread.

Despite all this, we're deathly afraid and we embody the "F" word—FEAR.

We resist traveling anyplace we've never been, because on those roads we don't know the way. We want a map, a compass, a GPS, but we forget that the richest roads are unpaved and unknown.

Maybe this is why *The Fellowship of the Ring* resonates with so many people. We see ourselves as common and unimpressive, just like the two hobbits Sam and Frodo. We fail to realize that our own courage can only poke through when we confront the unexplored.

Frodo heard the melody line before Sam and brought it to his attention:

> Sam: This is it.
> Frodo: This is what?
> Sam: If I take one more step, it'll be the farthest away from home I've ever been.
> Frodo: Come on, Sam. Remember what Bilbo used to say: "It's a dangerous business, Frodo, going out your door. You step onto the road, and if you don't keep your feet, there's no knowing where you might be swept off to."[9]

These two predictable hobbits needed to leave the "comfort of home," because that comfort was slowly killing them. There's nothing wrong with home, but if we're honest, most of us are strangers in our own homes.

We're homesick for a place we've never been.

Home isn't a bad place, but we often ask too much of it. We hope it answers all our aches. But home is a metaphor for where we've been, not a place we're going. Home can be a prison if it's a place devoid of growth.

Recently my "builder," Chet Scott, made a Deeply profound and Painful point to me. Chet is the founder of an unconventional company called Built to Lead.[10] Although some might try to label Chet a "life coach," he would beg to differ. Chet's heart is to build his clients by breaking them down—often through Pain.

During a chat, Chet pointedly observed, "You can't take the ring *and* stay in the Shire."

Ouch!

I wanted to do both simultaneously. I convinced myself safety and risk could be married. I believed comfort and adventure were compatible. Chet disagreed, and loved me enough to call me out. I needed to give up to go up.

This strategy requires confronting all kinds of Deep issues. Like failure, competence, risk, and reward.

The first place we need to travel is Deep inside ourselves—uncharted and untamed. Henry Stanley Haskins accurately observed, "What lies behind us and what lies before us are tiny matters compared to what lies within us."[11]

We need to feel our own Pain. And we must understand our own story if we hope to help other people find theirs.

So let me put it back on you.

What's your melody line?

Are you ready to take the ring?

Or do you want to just stay in the Shire?

3

The Door of Pain

Your pain is the breaking of the shell that encloses your understanding.

Khalil Gibran

I didn't go out looking for Pain. It found me.

I was a naive kid, some might say gullible, and I believed most everything people said. Why wouldn't I? The mean kids at my elementary school knew this quirk and loved exploiting it. They told me *gullible* wasn't in the dictionary, and I believed them. Their laughs felt like bee stings.

In second grade, I was waiting in line to get a drink from the water fountain, which in Wisconsin is called a *bubbler*.

Our teacher seemed distracted at the time and the kids took advantage by messing with me even more. Turns out I didn't know the meaning of many adult words. They asked me if I was a virgin. Ignorant of the meaning, I said no.

The only virgin I knew was Mary, the mother of Jesus. We'd say prayers to her in Mass every Wednesday morning at school. I'd look at her statue once a week and enjoy her peaceful smile. Funny how

33

she liked blue—always decked out in that color. I liked blue too, but other than that we didn't have much else in common.

I later found out I was a virgin, but by that time the kids had forgotten the joke and moved on to bigger words. Still, I never forgot the hurt in my heart, and unfortunately, with each passing year those bee stings got bigger.

I'll admit I didn't process Pain very well. Honestly, I never learned how.

Some people talk out their Pain. Others have thick skin and move past their Pain. A few shed their Pain when they shed their tears.

Me? I seemed to soak up Pain—every last drop.

For starters, I didn't like to cry. And talking it out was certainly out of the question. I had a severe stuttering problem and so my teacher, Sister Timothy, sent me to a special program with special classes for kids with learning disabilities.

I remember slapping my leg in order to get the words out. Call it a nervous habit or a coping mechanism, my intentional distraction made talking a tad easier. Focusing on my stinging leg meant no longer focusing on the sting from my stuttering.

The Pain of stuttering held my tongue hostage, and for some reason I couldn't untie it. "Think about what you're trying to say." "Focus in order to get the words out." "Slow down." Well-meaning adults tried their best to help by offering these and other quick-fix phrases. But their advice didn't help, and it only added to my problem.

I didn't need to think about speaking more—but less. I needed to distract myself and, lucky for me, I found a solution. Although I couldn't control my tongue, I had complete control over my hand. And strangely, I felt a little relief by slapping myself.

I didn't understand God's cruel joke—why everyone else talked so perfectly except for me.

Eventually, I just stopped talking altogether because words betrayed me and only invited more taunting. I wasn't a recluse, and the other kids probably accepted me more than I thought, but at that time in life I hadn't discovered my own voice.

I rather detested mine—a shaky, stuttering one at that.

⊓⊓⊓⊓

Chet asked me an interesting question a few years back. (He always asks the tough ones.)

"What's the universal emotion?"

Not quite understanding the question, I asked him to clarify. "You know, the one feeling that every single person has experienced?" he added.

It took me a moment to locate my answer. "Love," I suggested. "Everyone has experienced love."

But Chet kindly asked me to reconsider.

"Loneliness?"

"Nope."

"Fear."

"No."

"OK, then Pain. Every single person has experienced Pain," I proclaimed.

A smile slowly found its way onto Chet's face. "Exactly."

Think about it: Pain is the first feeling we express when we arrive in this world. And Pain is the last feeling most of us experience when we leave this world

If a baby *doesn't* come out crying, then medical professionals get worried and rush to discover the reason why the baby isn't expressing Pain. Chances are this lack of response is due to the reality that a Deeper Pain lurks beneath the surface.

Like a starving predator in search of blood, Pain smells us humans and hunts us down, unsatisfied until it satiates itself with our flesh. As long as we're breathing, we're vulnerable. And with each passing year I became an expert in Pain. Or maybe, to put it more accurately, I became addicted to Pain.

As a pastor in my final year of seminary, I aced the biblical text and its ancient languages. Comparatively, I failed to find a way of expressing my angst. Unable to find immunity from my increasing Pain, I masked it by wearing one. My plastic performance concealed the truth from everyone except myself.

I believed in lies: church leaders should have all the answers, God demands unquestioning allegiance, and my parishioners demand perfection.

Masking the Pain only made it grow stronger. Not about to come clean, I resorted to my learned coping mechanisms. Craving control over my Pain, I found a solution by carving my own skin. Creating a lesser Pain allowed me to manage my greater Pain. A professional in the pulpit, I protected my secret of self-injury and my addiction to fighting Pain by initiating more Pain.

Rather unconsciously, I used cutting to serve a strategic purpose. Much like hitting my leg in those stuttering episodes years earlier, self-injury distracted me from the Deeper issues that saturated my soul. If I couldn't control the Pain others inflicted upon my world, I'd control the Pain I inflicted on myself.

Like it does with every other human being, hurt kept finding its way into my heart. But unlike others around me, I couldn't locate the release valve. Some numb their Pain with substance abuse or irresponsible sexual experiences, but I saw the futility of both paths. I knew where they led—only into more Pain—and so I preferred one that left me calling the shots.

I turned my anger inward and unleashed that anger in calculated cuts. In those moments I felt control. With self-injury I decided how often, how Deep, and how long.

The author of my own Pain—my knife, the pen; my body, the pages—I found comfort in observing crimson words carved upon my skin. Inching closer to freedom in those perplexing moments, I desperately tried to dislodge my emotions buried Deep within.

Feeling like a stranger in my own skin, I didn't set out with the goal of self-injuring. I tried other ways of emoting such as capturing words with pen and paper, but the whole exchange left me unfulfilled. Unable to express the depth of my Pain, my writing made me feel like a pretender.

In my moments of emotional overload, I felt like a fraud in attempting to use words, knowing full well they simply weren't enough. My Pain was too Deep, my words were too shallow, and my anger was too intense. I needed to see red blood rather than blue or black ink.

Self-injury offered an escape that ensured me center stage in a complex dialogue I had exclusively with myself. The only privy parties to this discussion were my body and soul, for once both involved in the same conversation. With raw, unfiltered emotion rushing in, I embraced authenticity—even if only for an instant.

Odd, isn't it? A young man in his twenties, from a good home, trying to make a good home with his newly married soul mate and excelling in graduate school, with everything going for him—pastor, counselor, student, and teacher. Yet these titles couldn't take away the tension; these masks couldn't cover the hurt.

Many days I couldn't make it through without taking a blade to my body. My self-inflicted Pain distracted me from the Deeper Pain that had hijacked my heart. Odd?

No more so than the thin teenage girl who tries starving her Pain by starving herself. Searching for the perfect body buried somewhere inside her head, she needs more nourishment for her frail frame than food could ever provide.

No more so than the happily married man, the one with the loving and supportive wife and the kids who think the world of him, who hopes to muffle his Pain by gazing upon strangers posed in provocative positions. As if their sensual smiles could ever silence the ache that occupies his soul.

No more so than the older individual who sits alone, waiting to die. As they feel forgotten and invisible, their daily high points consist of opening mail and closing pill bottles. With nothing left to do and no one around to notice, their fantasies about funeral plans provide a small sense of purpose.

No more so than the woman in a lifeless marriage—the one who pretends by performing. But each passing year her forced smile seems less believable, and the kids have noticed the changing climate between Mom and Dad. Playing charades with her soul has taken its toll, and she's only one day away from blowing her cover.

No more so than the man who's recently been replaced. Slowly, over time, what he did became who he was and losing his job meant losing himself. Too tired to reinvent himself, he settles on settling and drifts Deeper into disillusionment.

No more so than the single mom who takes care of everyone but herself. Her cancer diagnosis cut much Deeper than her destructive divorce. Denying her death sentence, she tries killing the Pain by keeping busy.

No more so than the person on the receiving end of a bitter betrayal, the sincere friend who extended everything but gained only a bombshell in exchange as entrusted secrets shared in private are made public in a series of status updates. The allure of getting even through an unwanted digital dialogue promises a quick escape from the hurt.

Odd?

Maybe not.

Maybe it's human nature to avoid the ache and push away the Pain. Maybe some of us marry into the same dysfunctional system because it's familiar. Maybe we choose to stay in abusive situations because we know what's coming. Maybe we keep showing up at the same disengaging job because we fear the Pain of disconnecting. Maybe we self-injure because at least then we're the ones in control.

But maybe by numbing our Pain, we also sidestep our healing.

Experts insightfully warn us that insanity is doing the exact same thing and expecting different results.

So what if we changed our perspective on Pain? What if we stopped running and took the time to unwrap our Pain rather than avoid it? Maybe if we listened closer we'd hear something beyond the hurt.

Twentieth-century apologist C. S. Lewis believed that Pain is God's megaphone to wake us up out of our slumber.

Maybe God has been trying to use Pain in order to get our attention.

Maybe the answer to our ache exists underneath our Pain.

Maybe we need to dig a little Deeper below the surface.

And maybe by choosing the right Pain we will actually stumble upon recovery.

If you've never heard it before, let me be the first one to tell you: you are more than the Pain that defines you.

I know because I'm living proof. I'm more than a stuttering, insecure, self-injuring professional from the Midwest. When God looked upon me—in my moments of Deepest Pain—he saw more than the names carved into my legs.

People sometimes ask, "How did you stop cutting?" Although the answer is quite simple, the Path wasn't. The breakthrough occurred when I stopped avoiding my Pain and started exploring it. I entered the Deeper Path, and in that moment I unknowingly stepped closer toward healing.

While this book is about Pain, it's about much more than that. It's about pursuing that Pain all the way into our potential. It's about letting our hurts lead us to healing.

As long as I can remember, I've always loved stories. As a child one of my favorite storytellers, besides my parents, was my teacher Sister Timothy. Often I'd ask her to tell one of my favorite stories, which went something like this:

> Two rascally boys liked to cause trouble in a certain small town. They heard the stories about the old man down the hill. People said he was very wise, but they didn't believe it.
>
> One day they agreed to play a trick on him. On their way to his house they found an injured bird. Elated at their good fortune, they decided to test the old man's wisdom.
>
> They would knock on his door, and while holding the bird behind their backs they'd ask the man to tell them if the bird was dead or alive.
>
> If he said dead, they'd simply show him the injured bird.
>
> If he said alive, they'd crush the bird behind their backs.
>
> Either way, they knew they had him.
>
> Moments later, at the house, the old man gave his answer—an unexpected one at that. The old man told the two boys, "The answer is in your hands. It's yours to choose."

We all have a choice: abundant life or slow death.

What will you choose?

Based on my experience, I can say with great confidence that your Pain won't stop knocking on your door. Sometimes it's louder, other times quieter. But regardless, it's always there, lurking.

Eventually I got so frustrated I just opened the door and let my Pain come inside. I couldn't have imagined who would enter with it.

My potential.

These two visitors always travel together.

4

Leaving the Nursery

God whispers to us in our pleasures, speaks in our con-
science, but shouts in our pains; it is His megaphone to
rouse a deaf world.

C. S. Lewis

We never had one in our house. It wasn't the price that kept us away.
I think we just grew up without using them.

Although we had heard about them, it wasn't until six months ago
that my wife finally purchased one. Humorously though, after only
a week we ended up purchasing three more. And now we'd never be
without one—if we can steal them away from our kids.

Just the other day I came downstairs and saw our two-year-old
cuddled up in one. She's a smart girl who knows a good thing when
she sees it—or in this case, she knows a good thing when she feels it.

She loves her new electric blanket.

We live in Ohio, so at times the winter season can get a little chilly.
Now, with the flip of a switch, we get instant heat.

The bigger question is why we prefer a cozy environment.

Why do some people struggle to emerge from a warm, soft
bed devoid of noise and distraction? Why does 90 percent of the

population hit the snooze button . . . six times in a row? Why do we feel at peace swimming in a sea of sheets? Why does comfort keep us from activity?

When you were conceived, most likely you started in a warm, soft environment devoid of noise and distraction. Residing in a sac of safety and swimming in a sea of fluid, you were comfortably insulated and isolated. Your body felt the rhythm of your mother's, but for the most part you rested in your unawareness.

Eventually your birth day came and in Pain you entered a new world. Pain served as the catalyst for your new birth and propelled you from what you knew out into the vast unknown.

With each passing day Pain stalked you closely—the Pain of hunger, of feeling scared, of being alone.

Many of us experienced our parent's or guardian's desire to protect us from this Pain. As best as they could, they re-created a specific environment, better known as a nursery.

Nurseries vary in size and scope. Some are gigantic, outfitted with plush carpet and impressive mobiles. Others are quaint, painted with calming colors on all sides. Still, regardless of their size, most nurseries are designed with one specific goal in mind: safety. Baby wipe warmers, stuffed creatures, outlet covers, monitors, blankets, night-lights, cribs . . . all this Pain protection hardwired into our lives from an early age.

Thankfully, a few kind people took some measures of safety in your life. If they hadn't, you might not be reading this book at this specific moment, especially if they forgot those outlet covers.

But this desire for a Pain-free world doesn't go away later in life. No wonder as adults we feel at peace swimming in a sea of sheets, savoring that snooze button, sleeping without noise and distraction, and enjoying electric blankets. No wonder our warm, soft environment keeps us from activity.

There's nothing wrong with Pain-free experiences. Like most people, I enjoy the comforts of life. But the problem occurs when our aspirations rank no higher than insulating and isolating ourselves from Pain. The problem occurs when we become fixated on remaining in the nursery.

Adults were never meant to camp there.

We were meant for much more.

Our Creator knows the only thing that will propel us from the nursery. And if he didn't allow it in our lives, odds are we'd never choose it.

Good thing this one is not up to us.

I didn't wake up one day and decide to start carving cuss words into my arms and legs.

Life came fast, and with it Pain. When Pain comes knocking, we have two choices: to mask our Pain or to move toward our Pain.

The real kicker is Pain's uncanny ability to find us in the most inopportune times at the most inopportune places. A theoretically ideal setting with a theoretically ideal someone can just as quickly turn to mush in a matter of moments, simply because Pain decides to sneak in.

I remember back in college when Pain found me even though I disguised myself from it—literally.

A new transfer student on a new college campus, I arrived in Indiana without a car and without a care. Life decided to pack along some surprises in my suitcase, in addition to my unimpressive wardrobe. Back then I didn't thrive on the unexpected, but preferred words like *predictable*, *routine*, and *safe*.

Yet almost overnight a slew of fresh words visited my dorm, words like RA, RD, and in this case, RIP.

Prior to the semester starting, I thought RIP meant "rest in peace." Or more formally, RIP is an abbreviation for *requiescat in pace*, a short epitaph or idiom used to express wishes of eternal rest and peace for a soul that has died. How fitting.

This second definition would have peculiar implications on that particular night while I was on a relatively standard date with my girlfriend. No one literally died on our way to Fort Wayne, but *something* did at the rest stop only halfway into our trip. Truth be told, we never even made it to our destination that night.

This whole ordeal—asking your own girlfriend on a date—unfurled rather awkwardly. For three years now, our whole dating thing had been just part of the routine, but this RIP event rewrote all the rules.

"So . . . will you go out with me tonight, then?" I asked timidly, my voice trembling uncharacteristically over the phone.

I'm not quite sure why my nerves got the best of me—she was my girlfriend, after all. I guess the extenuating circumstances threw me off a little.

"Yes," the voice on the other end of the line replied confidently. "I'll go out with you."

"What time should I . . . you know . . . pick you up?" I fumbled, searching for the correct words.

RIP stood for Roommate Introductory Program, at least on this college campus. Don't ask me for an explanation or the evolution of such a program. Maybe it was the brainchild of a few desperate guys who couldn't get a date?

All I know is that this program existed for people who didn't have a boyfriend or girlfriend. Evidently, roommates understood their role as "matchmakers" and took the liberty of setting up their roommates on a date.

In my distinctive situation, going on a date with someone else didn't exactly make sense, so my roommate wisely set me up on a date with my own girlfriend—something I had done myself a hundred times before. Unwisely, he dialed her number and handed me the phone— thus the strained tone of our conversation.

"How about five o'clock?" she suggested. "At my dorm?"

We both lived in the freshman dorms. Me, the guys one. She, the girls. She, a legitimate freshman, two years younger. Me, a junior who'd just transferred. Both from the same hometown.

I walked onto this small college campus with last-minute over-tones—a romantic and a dreamer—too naive to know any different. The world was my ally—at least for a few more hours.

"Sounds good," I replied. "And just to keep things interesting with this whole RIP thing, I'll be wearing a disguise."

I hung up the phone with one hand and answered my roommate's high five with the other.

"Here it is," he stated, throwing me his Superman getup.

"I don't know," I questioned. "I'll give it a shot, but I feel stupid wearing it."

"Come on, man. Go for it," he said, reassuring me with a sincere smile.

"Yeah. Who doesn't like a guy in a Superman costume, right?" But unbeknownst to me, I'd soon encounter such a person.

Decked in blue tights and bearing a red rose, I boldly walked into her dorm. Immediately, I got a bunch of looks, but I only cared about hers.

Unfortunately, hers warned me something was Deeply wrong.

The quiet ride to Fort Wayne in my friend's borrowed car merely confirmed my hunch. Her abrupt request to pull over at the rest stop sealed the deal.

Evidently, my girlfriend felt like our three-year relationship had run its course. She wanted to end it and begin her college years without anything holding her back, including me.

I couldn't help but notice the irony of the whole evening.

Perfect outfit. In a Superman costume.

Perfect timing. On an RIP date.

Perfect place. At a rest stop.

Events in the parked car moved much too fast and I needed a breather. I sauntered to the men's restroom, Superman outfit and all. More than anything, I remember looking in the mirror, wondering what was next for me—knowing full well it didn't include another relationship.

I officially threw in the towel on dating.

Opening up my heart only produced Pain, and more than I could manage.

Although I wasn't a quick learner, time repeatedly taught me that getting close to people also meant getting close to Pain. The sudden death of a classmate due to cancer, the death of both grandparents, and the near-death of my brother from a drug overdose motivated me to build a fairly big wall around my heart. When emotions entered so did unpredictability, and so I simply made use of the emotional off switch.

I preferred an overcast environment accented with stoicism, devoid of any color. Functioning as a walking paradox and embodying a conflicted enigma, I made sure others couldn't get too close.

Part of me desired relationships, almost too much. I placed a great deal of emphasis on them, deriving my confidence and identity from them. But another part of me hated relationships. I believed they had the power to break me. Relationships removed my perceived control over life, leaving me vulnerable and fragile.

I justified my approach because it was safer and cleaner. Preferring transactional relationships instead of transformational ones, I tasted self-hatred for feeling weak enough to need relationships. I deceived myself into thinking that true strength meant independence from everyone else.

I disguised this divergence from everyone—and in a way, even from myself. Letting people in on the fact that I loved them only empowered them and their ability to hurt me, and so in order to function I just deprived them of knowing how much I valued them. I was locked in a Painful cycle of embrace and retreat, and such strategies came with a cost.

Like my secret about self-injury, for starters.

This twisted addiction seductively appealed to me—offering four impoverished promises:

1. The ability to be heard.
2. The ability to control.
3. The ability to punish.
4. The ability to feel.

Although emotions dressed themselves up as my enemy, like any other human I couldn't escape them completely. Self-injury allowed me the privilege of feeling, but in a setting I could control.

Most physicians agree that self-injury releases endorphins, a natural opiate-type feeling produced by the body. The Medical Dictionary informs us that endorphins are found in the brain and bind chiefly to opiate receptors in order to produce some of the same pharmacological effects (Pain relief) as those of opiates.[1] Even the etymology of the word *endorphin* (*endogene* or *endogenous*, meaning "growing within," plus *morphine*) reveals the potential power of these peptides.

Translation? Morphine on hand, opiates on tap.

I functioned as a person who felt safe living in a grayscale landscape the bulk of my time, and my self-injury allowed color to rip through, even if it entered predominantly with blood-red hues. When holding a knife I was intimately acquainted with authenticity for those brief moments and I no longer needed to hold my mask, but that hobby took what I call "soul toll."

When the stress of life hit dangerous levels of overload, I'd communicate my Pain by creating a lesser Pain. Cutting ensured my ability to emote, and seeing my scars validated the hurt Deep inside my heart.

Oozing with self-hatred, I directed my anger at my imperfections. Convinced that those around me required a flawless performance, I tasted my errors on a perpetual basis. My high standards mocked me with their toxic labels: Incapable. Failure. Loser. Idiot.

Some self-injurers cut straight lines into their bodies. Yet in my darkest moments I preferred carving words—degrading, profane, and cruel ones. Believing my body to be a blank canvas, I etched out my self-perception using crimson script. But despite my demand of payment for my shortcomings, branding myself only made the Pain fade temporarily.

Self-injuring is a chosen coping strategy for millions, and experts suggest four main reasons people do it:

1. To validate and express—Expression of things that can't be put into words (displaying anger, showing the depth of emotional Pain, shocking others, seeking support and help). Expression of feelings for which they have no label—a phenomenon called *alexithymia* (literally "no words feeling").
2. To self-punish—Because they believe they deserve punishment for either having good feelings or being an "evil" person. Because they hope that self-punishment will avert worse punishment from some outside source.
3. To control—In order to maintain control and/or to distract the self from Painful thoughts or memories.
4. To feel—Affect modulation. A distraction from emotional Pain: to end feelings of numbness, to lessen the desire to commit suicide, or to calm overwhelming or intense feelings.[2]

Why all this talk of self-injury, especially if it's not your specific hang-up? Because I believe by unwrapping self-injury, we inevitably unwrap ourselves.

Experts conservatively estimate that a staggering 1 to 4 percent of the general population and 15 percent of all high school girls self-injure.

But I believe that number is low, way too low; I believe 100 percent of us self-injure.

You see, all sin is self-injury.

We each utilize coping mechanisms in order to ease our ache: addiction to adrenaline and apathy to pornography. Illegal substances and illicit sex. Workaholics and shopaholics. Every coping strategy offers the same impoverished promises:

1. The ability to be heard.
2. The ability to control.
3. The ability to punish.
4. The ability to feel.

Our strategies might push away our Pain temporarily, but they also push away our potential permanently.

Thankfully, another option exists. By choosing our Pain, we can choose to step toward our potential and our ultimate healing— becoming fully alive. Think about it: the alternative to being fully alive isn't that attractive. It's numbness. Numb to emotion. Numb to feeling. Numb to life.

That's not a destination we set out to achieve, but it's one many of us settle for nonetheless. Life in the twenty-first century kind of demands numbness, doesn't it? We read global pandemic updates sent to our smartphones. We hear recession reports over our radio waves. We witness death splashed across our big screens. And all before a well-balanced breakfast.

We experience sharper anxiety even though we're more medicated. We feel greater loneliness even though we're more "connected." We taste Deeper hunger even though we're more fed. Maybe by "having it all," we realize how needy we truly are?

In 2006 IBM told us that by 2010 the amount of digital information would double every eleven hours.[3] What is that rate today, and who can wade through the plethora of information pollution?

Truth is, we feel the need to numb ourselves simply in order to survive. But unfortunately, we end up numbing more than we set out to. We crave an illusion, a life without Pain—but the price of such a life is also one without love, a truth realized by the character Lancelot in the movie *First Knight*. When discussing Lancelot's alleged lack of fear, King Arthur insightfully observes, "A man who fears nothing is a man who loves nothing; and if you love nothing, what joy is there in your life?"[4]

Love cuts Deep—much like a speedboat slicing through the sea. Sit in the back of the boat and you'll notice water rushing in to fill the space behind. Unlock the door to your heart and you'll discover that Pain—the unwanted stowaway—snuck in as well.

But consider—even *without* love comes Pain. If you're alive then you've felt Pain.

Despite this truth, we often attempt to rid our lives of Pain. This approach stems from several lies we believe that surround the topic of Pain. Here are a few of the most common ones:

Successful people have discovered the secret to eliminating Pain from their lives.

I should leave my organization or place of worship if it causes me any Pain.

Certain families have cracked the code on how to have a Pain-free home.

If my spouse brings me Pain, it's a sign that I married the wrong person.

If pursuing a dream causes me Pain, then I'm pursuing the wrong dream.

My sexuality is my own and my expression of it won't involve any Pain.

Gossip and complaining are productive ways for me to vent my Pain.

By inflicting Pain, I can distract myself from the Deeper Pain I feel.

Having perfect control over circumstances will help me avoid Pain.

Relationships or situations that bring chronic Pain can't be cured.

If I just had him, or her, or it, then I wouldn't have any more Pain.

A Pain-free marriage is possible and a goal I should pursue.

It's less Painful to invest myself at work rather than at home.

I can control people enough so they won't cause me Pain.

Buying on credit is a Painless solution to get what I want.

Substances and addictions help me cope with my Pain.

Having the perfect body will heal the Pain in my heart.

If I just made more money, then I'd rid my life of Pain.

If Pain must exist, then I should cope by masking it.

Movies and video games help me escape my Pain.

Eating food helps me starve the Pain from my life.

If someone causes me Pain, I should reject them.

Looking at pornography helps cure my Pain.

Human relationships shouldn't involve Pain.

A basic goal in life is to become Pain-free.

Christians shouldn't experience Pain.

If a job is a fit, it won't involve Pain.

A good God wouldn't allow Pain.

An affair will take away my Pain.

Good kids won't bring me Pain.

Exercise shouldn't involve Pain.

If we reduce these down to the lowest common denominator, the central lie we believe is this: Pain is bad and should be avoided at all costs. Lies like these go down easy because most of us don't have an alternative definition of Pain to challenge such beliefs.

Fortunately, the medical community offers one: "Pain is an uncomfortable feeling and/or an unpleasant sensation in the body. The presence of Pain often is an indication that something is wrong."[5] A few fascinating truths emerge from this definition:

Pain should be examined more closely in order to discover the Deeper issue.

Pain is merely an indication that something is wrong.

Pain shouldn't be avoided.

Pain isn't the problem.

Pain is a symptom.

This definition reframes the way many of us understand Pain. Most branches of society teach us the complete opposite—that we should avoid Pain because Pain *is* the problem. The medical community goes further by classifying Pain into two categories: chronic and acute.

Chronic Pain persists despite the fact that the injury has healed. Pain signals remain active in the nervous system for weeks, months, or years. Physical effects include tense muscles, limited mobility, a lack of energy, and changes in appetite. Emotional effects include depression, anger, anxiety, and fear of re-injury. Such a fear might hinder a person's ability to return to normal work or leisure activities. Chronic Pain might have originated with an initial trauma/injury or infection, or there might be an ongoing cause of Pain. However, some people suffer chronic Pain in the absence of any past injury or evidence of body damage.

Acute Pain begins suddenly and is usually sharp in quality. It serves as a warning of disease or a threat to the body. Acute Pain might be caused by many different events or circumstances. Acute Pain might be mild and last just a moment, or it might be severe and last for weeks or months. In most cases, acute Pain does not last longer than six months, and it disappears when the underlying cause of Pain has been treated or has healed.[6]

Within this conversation of Pain, more thoughts emerge that are critical if we want to understand more about ourselves and our world. First, most of us don't want Pain, but unless we learn how to deal with our Pain our only other option is to numb it. And regrettably we live in a world that numbs it well.

Second, all this Pain is an indication that something is Deeply wrong. Such Pain isn't good or bad—it simply *is*. Pain *becomes* good or bad based on what we do with it. Good Pain is essential and unless it's permitted, in many cases even pursued, then bad Pain will triumph and have its way.

Bad Pain: Extensive suffering that is chronic and purposeless. Bad Pain leads to a state of unproductive inaction and ultimately a type of serious injury or death.

Good Pain: Intentional hurt that is acute and purposeful. Good Pain leads to productive action and ultimately a type of healing or resurrection.

Think about your own life for a moment.

Which situations (relational, physical, emotional, spiritual) contain bad Pain? Which situations contain good Pain?

If we can't discern the difference, we'll tend to label them both negatively and dismiss them promptly, sending the good Pain packing. Two examples that distinguish the difference between bad Pain and good Pain can provide some clarity.

Physical Pain

Chronic back Pain is an epidemic in many parts of the world, including America. According to the American Chiropractic Association, thirty-one million Americans, or around 10 percent of the population, experience lower back Pain at any given time.[7]

Other facts related to chronic back Pain prove just as alarming:

Half of all working Americans admit to having chronic back Pain symptoms each year.

Back Pain is one of the most common reasons for missed work.

Back Pain is the second most common reason for visits to the doctor's office, outnumbered only by upper-respiratory infections.

Most cases of back Pain are mechanical or nonorganic—meaning they are not caused by serious conditions, such as inflammatory arthritis, infection, fracture, or cancer.

Americans spend at least $50 billion each year on back Pain—and that's just for the more easily identified costs.

Experts estimate that as much as 80 percent of the population will experience a back problem at some point in time.[8]

One solution for overcoming chronic back Pain is to develop a stronger core. Research reveals that, "weak or poorly controlled core muscles have been associated with low back pain."[9] By introducing acute Pain in the form of core muscle exercises (push-ups, sit-ups, planking, etc.), we can overcome chronic back Pain. By choosing acute Pain, we give our hurts the power to heal us.

In many cases, acute Pain might be nothing more than intentional exercise. One of the exercise programs I like is called the 3Ps—push-ups, pull-ups, and planking.

As a thirtysomething former high school wrestler, I've had my own bout with chronic back Pain. Two years ago the Pain climaxed and I found myself in the emergency room. One day after shoveling us out of a major snowstorm, I woke up at 4 a.m. in horrible Pain and was unable to feel my right leg. It turns out I had a bulging disc combined with weak core muscles that were aggravated by my abnormal shoveling stint.

I left the emergency room with two prescriptions for Pain medication and a suggested regimen of physical therapy. The medication immediately helped mask the Pain, but the real healing occurred by strengthening my core muscles. Two weeks later I found myself lying flat on a mat at the YMCA, stretching with my friend Kyle Schumm, a physical therapist. That day I introduced myself to acute Pain in order to overcome my chronic Pain. Although the therapy caused more Pain initially, it proved to be short-term.

Years later, I might occasionally detest my exercise routine—especially late at night after a long day at work and playing with the kids—but I detest skipping it even more. I'm a firm believer in regularly injecting acute Pain in order to overcome my chronic lower back Pain.

Similarly, in order to experience emotional and spiritual healing, we must also choose our Pain. When we inject the right kind of acute Pain we strengthen ourselves and our ability to overcome our chronic Pain. The path of recovery begins when we stop avoiding the ache and instead choose to explore, understand, and unmask our chronic bad Pain.

Relational Pain

Brian and I grew up together. He's got a lot of things going for him, and most women agree. He's never been married, but he says he'd like to be, with kids coming into the picture shortly thereafter. That is the vision he paints for himself, not for me or anyone else.

The crazy thing is that he's repeated the same Painful cycle since high school. He'll meet a wonderful woman with whom he shares much in common. They'll spend extensive time together, connecting on multiple levels. They'll have the same faith, the same dreams, and the same values. But without fail, they'll break up in about a year—maybe less.

The woman usually finds another man not long after and eventually gets married. Brian, on the other hand, will let a few months pass and then repeat the same cycle.

We—his family and friends—are exhausted from trying to keep up with the latest rendition of the same story. Our friend says he hates the Painful process too, but sure enough, after a little time has passed, he repeats the same cycle again. And again.

In the past, most of us spent our time trying to convince him that he needed to just take the plunge and get married. We labeled his problem "a fear of commitment" and used various strategies to help him overcome his fear.

We love Brian, want the best for him, and want what he says *he wants*. But after seventeen years, the story seems a little overdone. What if we fast-forward twenty more years? Where will he be then?

Recently, Brian and I connected over a holiday. Instead of repeating the same chronic, Painful conversation, I decided to change the tone. I injected a little acute Pain.

Rather than trying to convince Brian that he should get married, I took another approach. I tried to convince him that he *shouldn't* get married. I told him marriage was difficult and that his condition of singleness was very attractive. I highlighted all the wonderful freedoms included in his current life stage and then informed him about all the responsibilities of being a father and husband.

Instead of Brian defending the reasons he should stay single, as per usual, he actually rushed to explain the reasons why he *should* get married. The acute Pain I injected into the conversation—the Pain of staying single forever, against his wishes—briefly woke him out of the chronic Painful cycle he typically resides in.

But it wasn't enough, so I injected some more. Brian continued to defend himself. "I know the problem," he piously proclaimed. "The problem is that relationships stink."

After seventeen years of seeing my friend suffer, I knew he needed a strong dose of good Pain. Loving him, and not his approval of me, I spoke the truth in love. "No, that's too simple," I proposed. "Have you ever considered that *you're* the problem? Maybe it's not relationships that stink. Maybe *you* stink."

I didn't enjoy stating the truth or wounding Brian, but it had to be said. My friend's relational problem wasn't women, it was himself. Relationships were merely the context for him to see himself too clearly. By getting close to a woman, he got close to his own Pain, but rather than pursuing the Pain, he fled the relationship.

My strategy was simple: I tried to inject enough acute Pain that he'd wake up from his chronic Pain.

In the past, Brian would sit there and complain about his situation. His efforts produced nothing but extensive suffering and purposelessness. He existed in a state of unproductive inaction and, ultimately, serious relational damage—the exact definition of bad Pain.

So I switched the formula. I intentionally inserted a strong message that brought not only Pain but also purpose. I hoped it would lead to productive action and ultimately a type of relational healing and resurrection—the exact definition of good Pain.

But the choice of healing and resurrection isn't mine to make. It's entirely up to my friend.

We left the conversation with a clear decision that needed to be made. Rather than using the excuse of chronic Pain, which only produces chronic fog, he's now forced to deal with himself.

Does Brian want to overcome his issues that get exposed within relationships? Will he pursue the good Pain in order to overcome the bad Pain? Or does he want to continue in the same cycle? These questions now confront him. And whether or not he wants to, he must answer them. Life—and his current girlfriend—demand it.

Brian isn't all that unique. Many people weigh the cost of a relationship before committing to it. Many fear those bee stings in their heart and never open up because of that fear. Past hurts sometimes prevent future relationships.

Such was the case for world-renowned writer and professor C. S. Lewis. His mother's death from cancer when he was only a boy re-shaped his entire life. Pain walled him in, preventing Lewis from venturing into other relationships. He reasoned that a life of love meant a life of Pain, and regrettably he reasoned that such a life wasn't worth it.

Neither C. S. Lewis nor Brian were fans of the now-famous line from nineteenth-century poet Alfred, Lord Tennyson: "'Tis better to have loved and lost than never to have loved at all."

Lewis gained a prominent position as a professor at Oxford and held it for over thirty years, and within the academy he ruled the roost. His brilliant mind and keen humor ensured him the upper hand in professional encounters with colleagues and students. His intellect allowed him the ability to "school" any other educational opponent.

Lewis's books and writings became the context in which he explored other types of relationships. Within his fictional characters, he found complete control. His world of writing granted him godlike attributes: omniscience, omnipresence, and omnipotence.

But Lewis soon discovered that books can't talk back to you. Books can't embrace or engage you the same way a person can.

Just like my friend Brian, his need for relationships became too great. Eventually, love found him.

An American writer, Joy Gresham, came crashing into his life and brought love with her. Lewis and Gresham began a relationship and eventually married. Lewis felt alive and free, just as he did before his mother passed so many years prior.

But when Lewis opened the door of his heart to love, Pain snuck in as well. Only a few years into their marriage, Gresham suffered from the same disease that stole Lewis's mother decades before. When she died, so did a piece of Lewis's heart.

The movie *Shadowlands* captures this love story between Lewis and Gresham well. The emotional scenes include some incredibly insightful dialogue by Anthony Hopkins, who plays C. S. Lewis in the film. In one of those verbal exchanges, he brushes up against the Deeper Path.

Isn't God supposed to be good? Isn't He supposed to love us? Does God want us to suffer? What if the answer to that question is, "Yes"?

I suggest to you that it is because God loves us that He makes us the gift of suffering.

I'm not sure that God wants us to be happy. I think He wants us to be able to love and be loved. He wants us to grow up. We think our childish toys bring us all the happiness there is and our nursery is the whole wide world. But something must drive us out of the nursery to the world of others and that something is suffering.[10]

Within our lives, although we may crave the comfort of those cozy blankets, Pain is God's gift to push us out of the nursery. No wonder we feel unrest. We want healing, but we don't want hurt. We want love, but we don't want Pain.

And so we enter relationships with flimsy masks comprised of faulty demands and forced commands. We want a shadow of love, but we don't want authentic love. This is why it's so hard for us to understand God. We can't wrap our arms around how a good, all-powerful God can coexist in a world of Pain. We buy into a misbelief—that love can exist without Pain. But authentic love and Pain must coexist.

Authentic love led C. S. Lewis to care for Joy Gresham when she suffered from the same tragic disease that took his mother's life. Authentic love held Jesus's wrists to the tree as he took on the sin of the world. And authentic love serves as the glue in your relationships, despite the unavoidable Pain they contain.

But if we're honest, we still struggle. Knowing the truth doesn't make accepting that truth any easier.

May I ask?

Where are you still white-knuckled clinging to the illusion of the nursery? Where are you insulating and isolating your heart in order to avoid the hurt? How are you running from the relationship with yourself? With others? With God?

As a poster child from the nursery, I understand the logic of remaining there. It seems safer, cleaner, and more inviting.

But it's not. It's an illusion. And that's all it is.

You know this.

You taste this.

You feel this.

You've understood it for quite some time. This is what makes you different: the reality that you're willing to explore life outside the nursery. And this little difference sets you apart. But there's more to this little difference than what we can see.

We need to dig even Deeper below the surface. Let's find out together.

Shall we?

After you.

5

The Little Difference

You must strive to find your own voice. Because the longer
you wait to begin, the less likely you are to find it at all.

John Keating (Robin Williams), *Dead Poets Society*

I've always wondered what separates one person from the next.

In athletic championships, when adversity strikes one athlete rises
to the challenge and another athlete falters under pressure. In business setbacks, one leader rallies her department and another one
self-destructs. In economic difficulties, one family works together
under the banner of unity and another family fights each other and
goes down in flames.

The same team, the same organization, the same neighborhood,
but entirely different results.

In their book *212° The Extra Degree*, authors Sam Parker and Mac
Anderson expand upon this "little difference," referring to it as "the
extra degree."

"At 211° water is hot. At 212°, it boils. And with boiling water,
comes steam. And steam can power a locomotive. The one extra
degree makes the difference."[1]

The authors provide several other examples of "the extra degree" within the world of sports:

1. The margin of victory in the men's 800-meter race in the 1984 Summer Olympic Games was only 0.71 seconds—less than one second.
2. The average margin of victory in the Daytona 500 and the Indianapolis 500 (combined) over the last ten years has been 1.54 seconds. And the prize money for second place is less than half of that for first place.
3. The average margin of victory for the last twenty-five years in all major PGA golf tournaments combined was less than three strokes.[2]

Although these observations provide interesting trivia tidbits, the bigger question is the story behind "the extra degree." And even more relevant to our context: How is this degree quantified when it comes to people? It's one thing to win a race; it's another thing to overcome chronic personal Pain.

Bottom line: What can we credit for "the little difference"?

Some tip their hat to simple perseverance. Thomas Edison said, "Many of life's failures are men who did not realize how close they were to success when they gave up."

Examining Edison's life closer, we see a never-give-up attitude. As the story goes, Edison was asked why he failed so many times when trying to create the first lightbulb. He is famously quoted as replying, "I have not failed ten thousand times. I have successfully discovered ten thousand ways that it will not work."

Regardless of the complete accuracy of the story, we should question if simple perseverance was Edison's secret.

I don't buy it. It might read kindly in a greeting card, but you can't take it to the bank. Clichés don't convert into cash.

I bet people taught you the same warmed-over clichés they taught me. See if you can finish these statements:

1. No Pain, no _____.
2. Winners never quit, and quitters never _____.

3. If you can dream it, you can do _____.
4. No guts, no _____.
5. The early bird gets the _____.
6. It's not what you know, it's who you _____.
7. Be at the right place at the right _____.

Funny how much these phrases shape our ideology and direct our actions, many times even indirectly. Although a tiny nugget of truth might reside within each phrase, breaking them down reveals some interesting false assumptions.

1. No Pain, no gain.
    Key point: Hard work
    False assumption: Pain produces promotion.
    Truth: Choosing the right Pain produces promotion.
    Story: I know people who work incredibly hard, never reach their potential, and die with their music still inside them.
2. Winners never quit, and quitters never win.
    Key point: Persistence
    False assumption: Stick with something long enough and you will win.
    Truth: Healthy self-awareness of one's strengths and weaknesses combined with persistence can convert into winning.
    Story: I know people who never gave up their dream but failed to acknowledge they were completely unqualified to achieve it.
3. If you can dream it, you can do it.
    Key point: Imagination
    False assumption: Imagination guarantees you will achieve what you want.
    Truth: Vision is only the first step in possibly achieving what you want.
    Story: I know people who have an unlimited number of ideas that never amount to anything.
4. No guts, no glory.
    Key point: Risk

False assumption: Risk will yield reward.

Truth: The right risk at the right time in the right way with the right people will yield reward.

Story: I know people who take all kinds of risks and simply take recklessness with them wherever they go.

5. The early bird gets the worm.

Key point: Scarcity

False assumption: There is only one worm.

Truth: A mindset of scarcity, fear, and competition will produce a toxic attitude of threat and defensiveness.

Story: I know people who rush to take first and are in last place because of it.

6. It's not what you know, it's who you know.

Key point: Luck

False assumption: You can blame your plateau on a person you don't even know yet.

Truth: Before others will choose to believe in you, they will naturally judge if you believe in yourself.

Story: I know people who emitted the right frequency and attracted the right people to them because of it.

7. Be at the right place at the right time.

Key point: Chance

False assumption: You stumble into greatness when you stumble into the right space.

Truth: If you've prepared for the moment, then the moment is prepared for you.

Story: I know people who won while in the wrong place at the wrong time and others who lost when they were in the right place at the right time.

Although mining these myths proves helpful, it's still not enough. And if "the extra degree" even escapes these clichés, where can we find it? No one can deny its existence, but can we capture it long enough to examine it with the hope of mastering its genius?

⊐⊓⊓⊏

Sometimes this "little difference" pops through the surface when traumatic events pop into our awareness through the nightly news. One of these events occurred on an otherwise typical day in January 2011.

Although you might not agree with her public policies, if you heard her story your heart went out to Representative Gabrielle Giffords of Arizona, who survived an unexpected attempt on her life. Others were not so lucky. The shooter, Jared Loughner, killed six people and wounded thirteen more. Tragically, his youngest victim was a nine-year-old girl.

Because the shooter fired his gun from less than three feet away, sending a bullet straight through Giffords's brain, her future looked grim.[3] A portion of her skull the size of her palm had to be removed due to the swelling in her brain.

Grave predictions from professionals, like this one, surfaced rather quickly: "With guarded optimism, I hope she will survive, but this is a very devastating wound," said former surgeon general Dr. Richard Carmona, who lives in Tucson.[4] Severe brain injuries rarely produce anything but grief and tragedy, and less than 10 percent of people with brain injuries even survive.

But Gabby Giffords not only survived; she's also making a strong comeback. She and her husband, Mark Kelly, an astronaut and captain in the United States Navy, chronicled their painstaking journey in a book titled *Gabby: A Story of Courage and Hope*.

Mark lets us into their world when he vulnerably writes:

> I used to be able to tell just what my wife, Gabby, was thinking. She was a woman who lived in the moment—every moment. Gabby was a talker, too. Gabby doesn't have all those words at her command anymore, at least not yet. A brain injury like hers is a kind of hurricane blowing away some words and phrases, and leaving others almost within reach, but buried deep, under debris or in a different place.[5]

In Mark's own words, Gabby's voice was buried Deep and needed to be excavated. She wanted so badly to move on with life. She was lucky to be alive, but her recovery progressed rather slowly, at times making her feel less than lucky. Her life had changed dramatically and she couldn't just quickly move on.

In a real way, by losing her physical speech, Gabby also lost her figurative voice. She suffers from expressive aphasia, a disorder caused by damage to or developmental issues in anterior regions of the brain. Expressive aphasia blocks the ability to produce written or spoken language. Although sufferers cognitively know what they want to say, their brains cannot retrieve the correct words. Often frustration, grief, and depression set in.

But neither Gabby nor Mark has given up easily. Gabby is slowly finding her voice again, and ironically, it's directly tied to her finding her melody line, both literally and figuratively.

A Literal Melody Line

Given the nature of her story and the political ramifications involved, it's no surprise that in order to get Gabby back on track, Mark and other loved ones called upon many of the best experts around the world. However, one particular type of expert they chose might surprise you: a music therapist.

Singing in a time of overwhelming Pain? You bet. We can trick the brain by singing first and talking second. Music therapists tell us that when we sing we retrieve pitch, melody, and rhythm. Although language is normally held in the left side of the brain, music exists in both hemispheres.

"Music is that other road to get back to language," said Megan Morrow, Giffords's music therapist and a certified brain injury specialist at TIRR Memorial Hermann Rehabilitation Hospital in Houston, Texas. Morrow compared the process to a freeway detour. "You aren't able to go forward on that pathway anymore," she said, but "you can exit and go around, and get to where you need to go."[6]

Music helps many people get unstuck. Skeptically, some of us might wonder how someone can sing but not speak.

Dr. Oliver Sacks, professor of neurology and psychiatry at Columbia University, provides some insight. "Nothing activates the brain so extensively as music . . . and brain imagery . . . showed it had been possible to create a new language area on the right side of the brain . . . and that blew my mind."

Ever seen the movie *Awakenings*? Dr. Oliver Sacks's work with Parkinson's disease spurred both the film and eponymous book. He tells us, "These patients 'have some words somewhere,' but must be 'tricked or seduced into discovering them.'"[7]

Melodic intonation therapy (MIT) is the technical term for this therapeutic process used by music therapists and speech pathologists to help patients with communication disorders caused by brain damage. This method uses a style of singing called melodic intonation to stimulate activity in the right hemisphere of the brain, which assists in speech production.

MIT was inspired by the observation that individuals with expressive aphasia sometimes can sing words or phrases that they normally cannot speak. The goal of melodic intonation therapy is to utilize singing in order to access the language-capable regions in the right hemisphere and use those regions to compensate for lost function in the left hemisphere. Because patients are better at singing phrases than speaking them, the natural musical component of speech is used to engage patients' ability to voice phrases.

Notice the amazing pattern.

Gabby first finds her melody line.

Singing this melody line helps her remember her song.

And by remembering her song, she remembers her words.

And when Gabby remembers her words, then she rediscovers her voice.

In a literal sense, this process helps Gabby recover, but this process works in the figurative sense as well.

A Figurative Melody Line

Only weeks after Gabby's initial injury, Mark began presenting his wife with small goals, asking her how many fingers he held up or to recall simple memories. Mark believes hope is a form of love, and therefore, overcoming small challenges could produce small victories and with them small doses of hope.

As time marched on, so did their recovery from an incredibly traumatic event. Mark embodies courage on many fronts, including commanding the final mission of the Space Shuttle Endeavour less than five months after his wife's injury.

Asked to describe Mark in one word, Gabby chose "Brave."

Gabby embodies a bit of bravery herself. On August 1, 2011, less than eight months after the assassination attempt, she returned to Capitol Hill to make an appearance and received a warm bipartisan welcome from her colleagues on the House floor.

Having known much of her backstory, I sat stunned by the video footage of her appearance. Her "little difference" injected energy into the room that day. Electric and contagious, her courage did exactly what all courage is meant to do: inspire others.

Representative Jeff Flake said, "The two times that stand out in my mind—my whole memory of my time in Congress—is singing 'God Bless America' with people on 9/11 on the east steps [of the US Capitol] and then when Gabby Giffords walked in the chambers on August 1."[8]

How does someone in a matter of months go from speechless and sprawled out on a hospital bed to standing tall and speaking on the House floor on Capitol Hill? What is this "one degree" that sets Gabby Giffords apart from many other brain injury sufferers?

Unmistakably, it's because she found her voice. Watching her extensive interview with Diane Sawyer of *ABC News*, I learned that quite intentionally one particular phrase made it on her practice list for speech therapy: "I will return."

And herein lies another glimpse of the Deeper Path: her cross is bigger than her crown.

This is the same secret we observed in Captain Sully's ordeal earlier. And this is the same secret that enables me the privilege of writing you this book right now. Presently, one of these two orientations is pumping through your veins. Either your cross is bigger than your crown, or your crown is bigger than your cross.

You might not comprehend the magnitude of this subtle distinction right now, but you will. This "little difference" makes all the difference. In a manner of speaking, it is *the* difference maker.

Before we dig Deep into the cross and crown distinction, let's close the loop on Gabby. Like any good excavator, we want to know how it all turned out. Did she serve another term? Is she presently in office? How is she now?

Although Representative Gabby Giffords announced her resignation on January 22, 2012, she still clings to her crown. Intently, I watched the video in which she regrettably announced to her state and the world that her time in public office had ended. Here's what she said:

> Arizona is my home, always will be. A lot has happened over the past year. We cannot change that. But I know on the issues we fought for we can change things for the better. Jobs, border security, veterans. We can do so much more by working together. I don't remember much from that horrible day, but I will never forget the trust you placed in me to be your voice. Thank you for your prayers and for giving me time to recover. I have more work to do on my recovery so to do what is best for Arizona I will step down this week.[9]

She closed the video by saying, "I'm getting better. Every day, my spirit is high. I will return and we will work together for Arizona and this great country."[10]

That melody line, again: "I will return."

That's the same phrase we heard in her speech therapy. Because she clarified her crown and because she clings to that crown, she has the courage to carry her cross. Knowing the little bit that I do about Gabby, I'd say she's not setting that cross down anytime soon. Gabby understands the Law of the Crown: when we see our crown clearly, we can carry our cross willingly.

Her resignation shocked many who knew Gabby's resolve and determination. She embodied courage, and courage can't be contained because it's infectious.

Fellow Arizona Democrat Representative Raul Grijalva was surprised by Giffords's resignation. "I thought she would just see how the recovery proceeded, but I guess she decided in her own mind that this recovery is number one and that's the right decision for her," he said.[11]

Her growing fan club now carries her cross with her, and sometimes even for her. On days when she might not feel strong, her community fills in the gaps. This is the unavoidable byproduct of a clarified crown. People see it and, just as important, they hear it too.

Her melody line does the three things that all melody lines do:

1. Connects with people and taps into their Deepest values and aspirations.
2. Serves as the part of the song listeners remember.
3. Functions as the voice of her big idea.

We hear Gabby's song because we hear her voice. And many of us sing her song with her and for her, even in dark moments such as her resignation.

"She will fully recover and when she decides to come back from her pause to take care of herself, she'll pick up where she left off, there's no question about that," Grijalva said. "I'm looking forward to seeing her, thanking her, wishing her the best, and letting her know we're going to keep the seat warm for her."[12]

Gabby now embodies an idea much bigger than a political party. She transcended Congress and even politics by connecting with something every human faces: Pain. She models a lesson applicable to every soul who ever drew breath, and we would do well to understand the lesson and apply it in our own lives.

The Cross and the Crown

This concept first invaded my headspace when I watched the film *The Passion of the Christ*. Although the melody line came through clear, the application was a little foggy at first.

We hear the big idea within the dialogue between Jesus and one of the thieves crucified next to him. He obviously caught it too, based on his icy interrogation of Jesus.

"Why do you embrace your cross, you fool?" the thief spewed.

Good question.

Why would someone embrace something as Painful as a cross?

But it's just a movie, right? Make-believe? Jesus didn't really view his cross that way. Did he?

The Scriptures dispel the mystery for us. "Let us fix our eyes on Jesus, the author and perfecter of our faith, who for the joy set before him endured the cross" (Heb. 12:2 NIV 1984).

Joy about a cross?

Today, we beautify them. We wear them in our ears and around our necks. We see crosses in our places of worship and we find them within our art. We display them as a symbol of hope and inspiration.

Not so in the first century. Crosses were instruments of death. Crosses lined roadways, pathways, and walkways. They guaranteed certain sounds, like Deep moans of anguish from people suffocating to death. They brought undeniable smells, like the putrid stench of rotting corpses. And they invited certain images, like circling vultures that joyfully fed on decomposing flesh.

The Romans were smart people, utilizing crosses as motivation for accepting Roman control. They created them in order to inject a fear factor into their society. Visible, daily reminders to everyone, crosses depicted the result of rebellion, unconformity, and revolution. With the purpose of generating unquestioning allegiance, the Romans created the perfect killing machine.

Why would anyone welcome this instrument of suffering?

Today, it would be like expressing affection for an electric chair. I haven't seen too many people wear them as jewelry or portray them in art. And an electric chair hardly conjures up feelings of hope and inspiration.

But Jesus tapped into another reality. He saw the importance of the cross because he saw past it. He had crystal clear clarity for his crown. And he knew his cross was the only way to achieve his crown. So it became his passion and he carried it willingly, needfully, and even joyfully.

Experts generally define the word *passion* as a powerful and compelling emotion or a strong feeling or experience of love.[13] But surprisingly, the first definition for *passion* in Webster's dictionary is "the sufferings of Christ between the night of the Last Supper and his death."[14]

Even Mr. Webster heard Jesus's melody line. Jesus's passion connects so clearly with us that it shapes the way we understand the word itself.

Jesus's cross was merely a means to a much bigger end. His cross signified a step in the process. He didn't cherish the cross itself but what waited beyond the cross.

As the author of Hebrews writes,

Let us fix our eyes on Jesus, the author and perfecter of our faith, who
for the joy set before him endured the cross, scorning its shame, and
sat down at the right hand of the throne of God. Consider him who
endured such opposition from sinful men, so that you will not grow
weary and lose heart. (Heb. 12:2–3 NIV 1984)

The author exhorts us to consider the way Jesus approached his
cross so we will not grow weary and lose heart when carrying our
own. We are told not to focus on our cross, but rather upon Jesus as
our example.

Jesus embodies an idea much bigger than a religion. He transcended
life and even politics, modeling a lesson applicable to every one of us.
He embraced something every human faces—Pain.

ⅠⅠⅠⅠⅠ

So what about you? And what about your cross? More importantly,
what about your crown?

Go ahead and ask someone about their cross. Or if that word
doesn't connect, call it their "trial" or "Pain point." Just inquire into
what or who is bugging them. Most likely they'll give you a detailed
speech with sub-points and illustrations about all the struggles in
their lives. They are intimately acquainted with the unique nuances
of their cross.

However, ask these same people about their crown. Chances are
that when you do, you'll get a puzzled look. Most people are foggy
about it at best. And when we're foggy about our crown, then the
weight of our cross will soon crush us. Clarity when considering our
crown gives us courage when carrying our cross. One flows from the
other.

American businessman and author Max De Pree says, "The first
responsibility of a leader is to define reality."[15]

You might not accept the fact that you're a leader, or maybe you've
never even considered yourself one. But the truth is you're leading your
own life, whether your performance is stellar or poor. Responsibility
for leading our lives can't be placed on the government, the economy,
our businesses, our bosses, our friends, or our families.

If you want "the little difference" to emerge within your own life, then you need to question your condition. You have to be willing to turn down the noise and listen for the melody line emerging from your soul.

When you do, like Gabby, you'll find your voice.

And people want to hear it. Because when you have the courage to sing, you allow courage to do what all courage is meant to do: inspire others.

And we are a world in desperate need of inspiration.

PART 2

FEEL

The How

I've discovered that excavation is both a science and an art. As we continue to dig Deeper, I want to share some of that art with you. May it prepare you for our journey below the surface. You're about to encounter the Five Steps of The Deeper Path up close. Each step will take you closer to your Pain and your potential. Enjoy this poem as you head into this direction.

The Five Steps

Think about your own life for a moment.

> Take a Deep breath.
> Turn off your phone.
> Slow down.
> Tough?

Numb.

Notice your chest rising and falling.
Listen to the sounds around you.
Stop looking at your watch.
Focus on your breathing.
Take another breath.

Numb.

How long has it been since you have simply sat still?
Since you've walked barefoot outside in the grass?
Since you've plunged your hands into sand?
Since you've gone a day without technology?
Or just five minutes without it?

Numb.

When's the last time you rested?
Taken a True Sabbath?
For your mind?
For your body?
For your soul?

Numb.

When's the last time you made eye contact with someone?
The last time someone looked Deep into your eyes?
When's the last time you said "I love you"?
How does it feel?
How do you feel?

Numb.

When did you eat because you were honestly hungry?
And not because you were tired, anxious, or bored?
What's the last unexpected gift you received?
What did you do last week at this time?
Or yesterday at this time?

Numb.

Why are you rushing to get through this section?
What's more important than your soul?
What else do you need to do?
Why can't you just be?
Don't believe the label.

Numb.

Do you know yourself?
What's your Painkiller?
Your self-medication?
Your drug?
Your god?

Numb.

What are you running from?
Why are you running?
Who's chasing you?
Are you afraid?
Why?

Numb.

The choice is completely up to you.
It's your decision to make.
Move toward your Pain?
Or mask your Pain?
Feel?

Alive.

6

Step One

Question Your Condition

It's the question that drives us . . . it's the question that
brought you here.

Trinity (Carrie-Anne Moss), *The Matrix*

What annoys you?

Fingernails scratching on the chalkboard? Soup served cold when
you're famished? Important cell phone calls dropped?

Did I get your number yet?

Maybe for you it's not one of these but rather an empty toilet paper
roll when you're in desperate need of some? Or the feeling you get
when someone just stole your parking spot and you're running late?

Do any of these raise your stress level?

For me, none of these compare to my biggest stressor: being stuck.
I hate being stuck, because stuck stinks! Stuck is slow death and
chronic Pain.

Not only do I detest it, but I also loathe when other people are
stuck. The only difference between being stuck in a rut and stuck

in a grave is six feet. I like to see potential flowing smooth and free, unlocked and unleashed. I like to imagine the possibilities and taste the variety of options because I'm fueled by progress and adrenalized by production.

But I know the opposite too. I know plenty of people who are stuck. And I've not only seen the other side; regrettably I've taken up residence there in times past. I've camped in its courtyards and made my bed in its brokenness, most nights unconsciously. I don't think any of us willingly choose to be stuck. I believe we slip into it rather unintentionally. Given a little time, though, we become full-fledged residents. This doesn't excuse our condition; it only explains it.

Hang with me as I pull back the curtain a little. Psychologists call this "the four stages of competence" or the "conscious competence" learning model. The stages are:

1. Unconscious Incompetence
2. Conscious Incompetence
3. Conscious Competence
4. Unconscious Competence

Here's how it works. Everyone starts at a place of unconscious incompetence. We don't know what we don't know, because we're ignorant. Eventually some of us move to a place where we know what we don't know, a place of conscious incompetence. At this stage, at least we have a choice.

But many of us choose incorrectly.

We remain incompetent for fear of the unknown. We reason that with incompetence we're in control. Releasing control would mean bumping into conscious competence, but we fear letting go and focus more on what we might lose than what we might gain.

A few break free and stumble into a land of learning where everything is new and unfamiliar. Sure, mistakes arise, but eventually so do our levels of competence. Given enough time, those of us who become consciously competent, if we remain on the path of transformation, will eventually move to a place of unconscious competence and master the skills we once didn't even know we were ignorant of.

To better understand, try on this example.

At one period in my life I didn't know how to drive a car. When I was really young, I didn't know that I didn't know. I simply sat in the car as a passenger, completely clueless that someday I might drive one. I was young, ignorant, and comfortable.

But time marched on.

I grew up and so did my friends. One day, my friend's older brother mentioned getting his temporary license. I slowly became conscious of my incompetence. I knew I didn't know how to drive a car, but that day I vowed that one day I would. I made it my goal to move from conscious incompetence to conscious competence.

I began to study for my temporary license and to watch how other people drove. I listened to their reactions and I observed their habits. Eventually I took a driver's education class and sat behind the wheel for the first time. I moved from being stuck to unstuck.

Over time, I mastered the skill of driving.

I eventually arrived at the place I currently reside—a learned model of unconscious competence. I now occasionally drive entire trips across town without even consciously thinking about it. My eyes move from rearview mirror to driver's side mirror and my hands remain in their proper position. I can even engage in a conversation with passengers or on my cell phone via a hands-free device.

My mind, my emotions, my body, and my spirit all unite in a time and space and operate with intelligence in an unconscious effort to achieve one particular goal. Not only do I benefit, but the passengers with me do as well. We all arrive safely at our intended destination.

As humans, our natural progression flows from unconscious incompetence to conscious incompetence to conscious competence to unconscious competence.

Or for the visual learners, picture this:

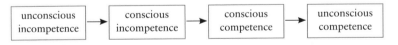

Although a learning model like this packs endless potential, the real key lies in moving from level 1 to level 2, or from ignorance to choice. When we're aware we're stuck, then we have options. We can stay there, and many do, or we can take the Deeper Path and move toward becoming unstuck.

But when we lack the self-awareness that we're stuck, it's highly unlikely we'll ever become unstuck. Just try to help an ignorantly stuck person and you'll often catch a large helping of anger and misunderstanding, such as in these three examples.

One: Consider Physical Health

Imagine suffering from abnormal weight loss and stomach pains. Now imagine someone telling you that you can't eat any gluten. My brother can't eat gluten and his condition drastically affects his eating experience. Look at food labels sometime. Gluten finds its way into a whole bunch of items like wheat (including kamut and spelt), barley, rye, malts, and triticale. My brother has to choose certain restaurants based on their menus regarding gluten.

The average person wouldn't eliminate gluten from their diet simply because someone told them to. But imagine if a doctor, through a series of testing, diagnosed you with celiac disease. Now imagine you saw the test results.

Because you moved from unconscious incompetence to conscious competence, from ignorance to accountability, you now have a choice. If you ignore the test results you will have to pay up. According to Celiac.com, if someone with this disease continues to eat gluten, studies have shown that he or she will increase their chances of gastrointestinal cancer by a factor of 40 to 100 times.

Self-awareness comes with a cost. But ignorance does too.

Two: Consider Parenting

It's a whole lot easier giving your kid help when they realize they need it. And it's even better when they ask for help. But what if that same kid never realizes they need help? What then?

Can they ever be helped?

Not very easily.

What if you and I resemble that kid in more ways than we think?

How would we know? What if there are certain areas in our lives where we don't know what we don't know? What if we don't realize we're stuck?

How can we escape our unconscious incompetence and gain the self-awareness needed to see ourselves clearly?

Three: Consider Movies

Agent Smith unwrapped this phenomenon further in the movie *The Matrix*. He commented on the complexity of the Matrix. "Have you ever stood and stared at it, marveled at its beauty, its genius?" he said. "Billions of people just living out their lives, oblivious."[1]

In the film, the unconscious incompetence of humans gave sentient machines their edge. These machines depended on humanity's ignorance of their condition. These machines pacified the population with electrical impulses meant to distract them from the real truth: that they're stuck, serving the machines unknowingly.

Unfortunately, when we don't know what we don't know, why would we ever change? When we lack the self-awareness that another way even exists, how could we choose another option?

Morpheus understood this point and expounded to his protégé Neo.

"The Matrix is a system, Neo. That system is our enemy. But when you're inside, you look around, what do you see? Businessmen, teachers, lawyers, carpenters. The very minds of the people we are trying to save. But until we do, these people are still a part of that system, and that makes them our enemy. You have to understand, most of these people are not ready to be unplugged. And many of them are so inured, so hopelessly dependent on the system, that they will fight to protect it."[2]

Sound familiar?

Sounds to me like the same kid who needs help but doesn't know he needs help. Sounds to me like the kid who sees her parent as the enemy, not the ally. Sounds like someone who's stuck but doesn't know it.

Morpheus continued to explain the gravity of the situation. "Have you ever had a dream, Neo, that you were so sure it was real? What if you were unable to awake from that dream? How would you know the difference between the dream world, and the real world?"[3]

Morpheus warned Neo that ignorance isolated and insulated people from their ability to see themselves objectively. Those of us who know the storyline of the film know that Neo faced a choice: Would he risk his life to save the same people who longed both to kill him and to save the very system that enslaved them?

Sounds like another familiar story. One about a certain first-century rabbi who hung on a cross and said, "Father, forgive them, for they know not what they do."

So how can we get unstuck if we're not aware we are stuck?

If we pay closer attention to the words we use, our vocabulary might just give us away.

Here's why.

We tend to use linguistic metaphors to explain the way we see ourselves. When we feel "up," we use phrases like:

I am on top of the world.	I am invincible.
I am unstoppable.	I am on a roll.
I am bulletproof.	I am on fire.

But we use other phrases when we feel stuck. We say things like:

I am missing a piece of the puzzle.

I am in the wrong frame of mind.

I need to think outside the box.

I am going in circles.

I can't snap out of it.

I am stuck in a rut.

These last six metaphors express a low level of awareness that we are stuck and powerless.

First we think it.

Then we feel it.

Then we say it.

And then we live into it and from it.

The cost of living from those phrases will take a toll on you and those around you. When swimming in this type of headspace we often devote our awareness to our problems and end up losing touch with our own resourcefulness. In America alone much of the population feels stuck, held back, and detached from their own resourcefulness:

1. One-third of Americans are struggling to live to their "fullest potential."
2. Nearly seventy million Americans are dealing with emotional conflict.
3. Seventy million Americans feel held back by their past.[4]

French-born American author Anaïs Nin wrote, "We don't see things the way they are, we see things the way we are."[5] Whether or not we agree with this reality, we're an extension of our world. When we're off-center, perplexed, or conflicted, then our world is as well.

We question our own power and ability to create and grow. We operate out of scarcity instead of abundance and become takers instead of givers. We only see what we're not and we often become angry and frustrated. We crack open the door and let fear creep in. But thankfully, if we're self-aware, we also recognize a longing.

We become aware of a brighter future and a better possibility. Something in us awakens. We want to create a life that truly resembles what we believe is possible. We don't want to stay stuck anymore. We want to be more, have more, do more, and give more.

We want to grow. Our spirit, the most powerful part of us, speaks to us. Our spirit, the space where we give and receive signals to and from God, reveals a greater reality.

We feel called to a higher expression and a fuller expansion of our current awareness and achievement. Our spirit speaks to our soul through our discontentment and longing. And although these emotions might seem like uninvited guests, we should welcome them.

Remember, dead people feel nothing. No pleasure or joy. But also, no discontentment or longing. Nothing.

Celebrate the reality that you feel something, even if it is unpleasant at the moment.

The fact that you feel is proof you're alive.

Saint Augustine wisely exhorted, "If you would attain to what you are not yet, you must always be displeased by what you are. For where you are pleased with yourself there you have remained. Keep adding, keep walking, keep advancing."[6]

Although his quote brings encouragement, it also brings admonishment. In order to feel the full weight of our potential, we first need to feel the full weight of our Pain.

And to do this, we have only one option.

We must first unmask our Painkillers.

7

Step Two

Unmask Your Painkillers

We'll try and ease the pain but somehow we all feel the
same.

Smashing Pumpkins

Our wise friend Pascal uttered these words of life hundreds of years
ago: "I bring you the gift of these four words: I believe in you."

The first time someone gave me these four words sincerely, from
their heart, I was a young man in desperate need of belief. These
words altered my life, gave me wings, and changed the trajectory of
my future.

Strangely, we're the last person to see our own potential. I'm quite
certain that, at this exact moment, you don't see your full potential.
But I do. Grant me the privilege of possibly being the first person
ever to express the truth: I believe in you. And I want you to achieve
all that you've been created for.

But in order for you to do so, I'm going to have to inject a little
acute Pain into this chapter.

Remember the conversation I had with my friend Brian about relationships? It originated out of love. I care Deeply about my friend and want to see him grow. That's the only reason I challenged him.

Likewise, this chapter contains a little tough love. It's the only way I've grown and it's the only way I continue to grow. I have a few truth-tellers in my life. I know they love me because they care more about my growth than my temporary happiness. They practice Emily Dickinson's insight, "Truth is such a rare thing, it is delightful to tell it."[1]

Sometimes they're pretty direct with me. Other times they throw a challenge my way. Bottom line: they help me go faster and further. And so I'd like to throw a little challenge your way. If I have your permission, keep reading.

⊥⊥⊥⊥⊥

I dare you to do something.

I bet you can't do it because, like me, you've been hardwired and conditioned not to do it. Why, you may ask?

Well, that's a difficult question to answer. Maybe it's because we've been trained that it's wasteful or lazy. But those are probably just excuses. So let's dig a little Deeper and take another step.

I think you're addicted. (I know I am.)

I'm not referring to an addiction to substances or sex. It's an addiction to something much more subtle.

Noise. We all crave noise.

Hundreds of years ago Pascal saw this tendency, even before TiVo, or movies, or electricity. He wrote, "All of man's difficulties are caused by his inability to sit quietly in a room by himself."[2]

You might be thinking, *Really? All of our difficulties are caused by a lack of reflection that results from an addiction to noise?*

I encourage you to take a shot at my dare. Go sixty seconds. Shut off everything you can. Your phone, your music, your TV. Whatever is on. If it has a switch, turn it off.

You might struggle in accepting the challenge. But here's the truth. If it's not that big of a deal, then do it. Take one minute and invest in yourself and your potential. Take one minute to unmask your Painkiller.

Sit still for sixty seconds. Hit pause and close your eyes.

(Sixty second pause.)

If you took the challenge: What did you think? What did you hear? What did you feel? Try to verbalize your experience. Journal your thoughts.

OK. Now that you're warmed up, I'm going to step it up. Now try five minutes. Maybe you're thinking, *Five minutes? What?* Let me ask: When's the last time you sat in silence for five minutes?

One day?

One week?

One year?

One life?

Trust me. This will give you greater clarity. Try five minutes of silence. Hit pause and close your eyes.

(Five minute pause.)

Again, verbalize your experience: What did you think? What did you hear? What did you feel? Try to describe your experience. Journal your thoughts.

Turning down the noise helps us to think better. And we all know that most people don't think. Thomas Edison said, "Five percent of the people think; ten percent of the people think they think; and the other eighty-five percent would rather die than think."[3]

We prefer amusement instead. But consider the word *amusement* and its etymology for a moment.

A = Not

Muse = Think

Amusement = Not Think

Amusement means "to distract or divert." What if I told you that amusement was distracting and diverting you from your potential?

Most of us would admit it . . . and then do nothing. You see, it goes back to the cross and crown analogy again. If we can't see our crown then we will numb our cross with noise.

But try on this illustration. What if I told you a loved one was in a car accident and was hanging off a bridge only a block away? Would you delay by distracting yourself with amusement?

Of course not. You'd drop everything to pursue something of greater value—your loved one.

But what if the example changed a little? What if you couldn't hear me when I told you about your loved one? What if you were too distracted?

Let's make it personal, within our conversation:

What if all you can see is your cross?

What if you can't see anything of greater value?

What if you don't know what you love?

What if you can't identify your crown?

No wonder we so often crave noise. It numbs us from these questions. And unfortunately, noise comes in many forms, including relationships with others. For example, why do we default to others when we need advice? Why do we seek out their noise before we even consider an answer for ourselves? Many of us are addicted to other people's opinions. Apple founder Steve Jobs warned us about this tendency:

> Your time is limited, so don't waste it living someone else's life. Don't be trapped by dogma—which is living with the results of other people's thinking. Don't let the noise of others' opinions drown out your own inner voice.[4]

Counselors, coaches, teachers, pastors, trainers, friends, and family can all contribute their experience and insight into our situation, but at the end of the day we're responsible for the action (or inaction) we choose.

Noise only contributes to the fog if we don't first take the time to be silent.

This internal work must be done before our defining moment arrives. Remember our friend Captain Sully? He did his hard work before the bird strike. When opportunity unveiled itself, he could act immediately because his mind was clear.

Bono recognizes this, and believes the common thread between great leaders is their "ability to see through the din and clangor of ideas and conversations and points of view, and hear the melody line, and realize: this is the thing we've got to do, this is more important than the others."[5]

Noise will come; it's inevitable. But if we do our soul surgery before the crisis, then when the choice comes we will be ready. When we prepare for the moment, the moment is prepared for us.

In my work of helping people, I recently met a middle-aged woman named Rose. Rose is addicted to Painkillers. But she's not that different from the rest of us. We all engage in what *The Grief Recovery Handbook* calls S.T.E.R.B.S., or Short Term Energy Relieving Behaviors.[6]

Although the flavor of Painkiller varies from person to person, each Painkiller has one single, obvious goal: to kill Pain.

Here are just a few examples:

Romance novels	Success
Extreme sports	Church
Video games	Money
Substances	Work
Busyness	Sex
Shopping	TV

The list could go on as long as people are alive in the world. But rather than discuss an endless list of Painkillers, I'd like to emphasize a practical strategy in helping to unmask them. Remember, we can't change what we're not aware of. But thankfully, when we're aware of something at least we have the option to change.

First let me give you a little background on Rose:

Her ex-husband left her ten years ago with $10 and a mortgage payment.

She stayed with her abusive husband longer than she should have.

She has been admitted to the hospital for psychiatric evaluation.

She's addicted to her Painkiller of choice: self-injury.

She can't make it through a day without cutting.

She believes she's too unworthy for God.
She's a single, divorced mother of seven.
She's scared to attend church.
She's lost her job.

A Practical Strategy

After Rose explained the details of her self-injury, I asked her to unmask her Painkiller. She fearfully replied, "What do you mean?"

"Rose, I'm going to ask you to switch strategies. I'd like to ask you to try something else the next time you want to cut." I continued, slowly and respectfully, "I'd like you to write your own psalm."

"My own psalm?" she immediately responded. "What's that?"

I then went on to tell her about a certain group of psalms in the Bible called the "imprecatory psalms."[7] This particular group causes most theologians to squirm in their seats.

According to *Theopedia*, an encyclopedia of Christianity, the imprecatory psalms contain curses or prayers for the punishment of the psalmist's enemies. To imprecate means "to invoke evil upon, or curse."[8]

These psalms are written by David, a king of Israel, someone the Bible identifies as a man after God's own heart (see Acts 13:22). The Bible holds up David as an example to emulate.

Because the Bible gave him this label, you might think his psalms would be sanitized and Pain-free. A few might match that description, but certainly not the imprecatory ones. These ancient writings are chock-full of struggle, tension, doubt, anger, revenge, hurt, and fear.

I love them because these psalms saved me back in my Painkilling days. They breathed life into me, and I saw hope in them.

Here are a couple of my favorite passages:

> Save me, O God,
>   for the waters have come up to my neck.
> I sink in the miry depths,
>   where there is no foothold.
> I have come into the deep waters;
>   the floods engulf me.

> I am worn out calling for help;
> > my throat is parched.
> My eyes fail,
> > looking for my God.
> Those who hate me without reason
> > outnumber the hairs of my head;
> many are my enemies without cause,
> > those who seek to destroy me. (Ps. 69:1–4)

> Pour out your wrath on them;
> > let your fierce anger overtake them.
> May their place be deserted;
> > let there be no one to dwell in their tents.
> For they persecute those you wound
> > and talk about the pain of those you hurt.
> Charge them with crime upon crime;
> > do not let them share in your salvation.
> May they be blotted out of the book of life
> > and not be listed with the righteous.
> But as for me, afflicted and in pain—
> > may your salvation, God, protect me. (vv. 24–29)

Can you believe David's brutal honesty? I couldn't the first time I read these verses. How could a man after God's own heart ask God to blot out his enemies from the Book of Life because he's in Pain? I've never heard these psalms preached or sung in church before. I wonder why. Here's another one:

> Appoint someone evil to oppose my enemy;
> > let an accuser stand at his right hand.
> When he is tried, let him be found guilty,
> > and may his prayers condemn him.
> May his days be few;
> > may another take his place of leadership.
> May his children be fatherless
> > and his wife a widow.
> May his children be wandering beggars;
> > may they be driven from their ruined homes.
> May a creditor seize all he has;
> > may strangers plunder the fruits of his labor.

> May no one extend kindness to him
> > or take pity on his fatherless children.
> May his descendants be cut off,
> > their names blotted out from the next generation.
> May the iniquity of his fathers be remembered before the
> > LORD;
> > may the sin of his mother never be blotted out.
> May their sins always remain before the LORD,
> > that he may blot out their name from the earth. (Ps.
> > 109:6–15)

After reading these psalms, I reasoned that if a man after God's own heart could be this bold and raw, then there must be a place for me at the table. You see, up until this point I believed God didn't want to interact with me unless I was happy, calm, pleasant, and perfect. I believed I could only come into God's presence all cleaned up.

So guess how long I waited to come to God?

A very long time. In reality, I never came to God, at least not in the way I should have. When we think something other than God can clean us up, then we're believing a lie. But that's the exact strategy of the Enemy of our potential. He wants us to believe we can't come to God until we're perfect.

I would still be waiting today.

And you would be too.

Maybe you still are.

In those days of plastic performance I practiced something I call the "Holy Heisman." If you're a football fan you might understand. I'll explain.

The Heisman trophy is an annual award given in college football. The statue depicts a player with one hand out in front, pushing opponents away, and the other hand placed near his heart, guarding the football.

In my relationship with God, I practiced the "Holy Heisman" position. I had one hand in front of me, pushing God away with my tasks. I reasoned that as a pastor I could keep God at bay and satisfy him with my good works. I figured he'd be pleased with all the work I did for him, or at minimum he'd get off my back and leave me alone. I preferred to live my life and expected God to live his, with us hooking back up in the afterlife.

I placed my other hand over my heart to guard it. I wasn't about to let God get close to me, and so I desired a transactional relationship with him rather than a transformational one. Although I associated myself with him, I wanted to keep him at a distance, where I could control him.

Many of us have a rocky relationship with our heavenly Father, perhaps due in part to rocky relationships with our earthly father-figures, or lack thereof, or at least the ones we observe plastered across movie screens. Sometimes, we can see the latter with more clarity because our issues don't get in the way. I think you'll recognize this particular example from the movie *The Lion King*, a story about a lion cub who struggled a bit with his father.

Rather quickly, we meet Mufasa, king of the jungle, ruler over all. In the beginning he and his son, Simba, had a beautiful father-son relationship. The world seemed perfect, or so Simba thought.

As he got a little older, he listened to the voice of his deceiving uncle Scar and trespassed into a forbidden place—the elephant graveyard. Sensing Simba was in danger, Mufasa sacrificed his own life to save his son.

Immediately, guilt plagued Simba and he fled, ashamed of his foolish choice that cost his father's life. As time marched on, Simba forgot who he was and lived a life of purposelessness instead.

His kingly father became a distant memory, not a daily reality. Simba saw himself as an embarrassment, no longer worthy to be called a child of the king. Finally, after running for years, he reached the end of himself and vulnerably cried out to the heavens, "You said you'd always be there for me, but you're not . . . it's because of me . . . it's my fault."

The moment he was finally honest, his breakthrough came via a crazy messenger. The monkey Rafiki confronted Simba in the midst of his identity crisis and led him through the jungle, to a pond where he saw his father's reflection. Simba finally poured out his heart to his father.

He confessed his inadequacies, his shortcomings, and his hang-ups. His father listened, but then spoke boldly. "You are more than who you have become . . . remember who you are."[9]

Mufasa reminded him of his position—who he was, not his condition—how he was.

When Simba poured out his heart to his father, only then could he embrace his true identity and accept the crown that was rightfully his.

⊥⊥⊥⊥

This is the journey I invited Rose to take. I asked her to pour out her heart to God. I asked her to be real and raw and tell God whatever she felt, even if she thought it was disrespectful or sinful. I asked her to vulnerably cry out to the heavens.

She was scared at first. But with a few more promptings she eventually did. Here is her psalm to God:

Dear God,

I am writing to keep myself from cutting. Every time I cut I get madder and madder. I like cutting because it makes me feel better, but I know I need to find a different way to express what is inside me. I have been hiding behind masks for too long. You know what's in there already so please help me to understand it. I know you have a better name for me than the names I carry around.

You know that each cut has a name; and you know what they are: loser, wreck, shameful, reprehensible, stained, abandoned, destroyed, unworthy, filthy, stupid, hideous, fat, grotesque, disgraceful, bad, incompetent, dumb, disgusting, hated, phony, deceiver, insignificant, failure, unlovable, ruined, insufficient, fearful, anxious, nervous, cutter, unwanted, alone, disguised, masquerade, angry, imperfect, empty, defective, abused, and appalling to name a few. Why have you left me abandoned? Why do I feel so empty inside? Why do I feel like your grace is not Deep enough for me? Why do I feel like no matter how many times I say the salvation prayer I am still not saved? Why am I so angry with you?

Why did you leave me in a marriage for seventeen years that was abusive physically, mentally, verbally, and sexually? Why did I stay and let him abuse not only me but the kids? They were just babies and the physical and verbal abuse they had to endure was appalling. I took them to church every Sunday and they learned about a kind and loving Father, and then I brought them home and they learned something else. Why didn't I get out sooner? They were just babies and I had to send them to school in turtlenecks to hide the bruises.

Why did you leave me for ten years alone as a single parent? I could barely handle being a single mom and now I was mom and dad. I failed you miserably for that. Looking back I can see that we had what we needed, more than we needed, so for that I say thank you. I was always worried about where the next money was going to come from but somehow it always worked out even though there was so little of it.

Why did you allow me to work so hard to get a full-time teaching job and then yank it out from under me? That happened four years ago and I am still just as mad and hurt as the day it happened. I don't understand WHY. WHY? WHY? WHY? I did everything I was supposed to do and you took that away from me. . . .

I don't understand why it is so hard for me to be real with people. I always say everything is fine, and inside everything is a jumbled up ball of muck and I feel alone and abandoned and fake and phony. I want to get this muck out of me so I can be the authentic person you have called me to be.

But I'm angry. I'm angry that I had to be locked up in some mental hospital and that it takes me twenty pills a day just to be able to survive in a somewhat normal way. But more than that God, I'm angry at you. I don't understand. I don't understand why.

I understand that I am at the end of my rope and don't have anywhere else to go or anywhere else to turn. I'm broken, I'm empty, and I need you to come to me in a very real way. I don't know what that means or what it looks like, but I know I have nothing else to give right now. I have tried it my way for so long. I ran off the road and into the ditch so long ago I don't know if it will come out. I am sorry that I have struggled with the sin of pride for so long.

I am asking for forgiveness and please take it from my life. I'm tired and I'm weary and I can't do this anymore. I can't keep pretending that I'm something I'm not. I am an insignificant failure and I am ashamed. Thank you for all the blessings that

I have been too blind to see. Thank you for my seven beautiful children and for my granddaughter. Thank you that your granddaughter has a better earthly father than my children did.

Please come and fill my brokenness and help me not to cut or want to kill myself anymore. I'm sorry that I'm mad at you and that I blame you for what I really did.

Both Rose and I were a bit surprised at how easily the words came. It's almost as if they were on the tip of her tongue, just waiting to come out. But up until this point she had chosen to express them with a knife on her body.

I've noticed an interesting pattern. Once people begin unmasking their Painkillers they usually gain new courage. They begin to feel stronger and bolder because they realize another path is possible.

Here's one more of Rose's psalms. Notice the clarity beginning to surface.

What is hiding deep inside
  I don't even know
  I'm trying hard to figure it out
    and not to let fear show
  The pills the cutting the negative talk
    or sleeping all day long
    they're all just things I use to cope
    so it just goes on and on
  I want to throw those things away
    and step into the light
    the fear is paralyzing me
    the light seems way too bright
  Even though I know the light's the only way
    and the only way I'll get there is walking day by day
    what happens if I take the step out into the light
    what if the light rejects me and throws me back into the
night

Each time Rose engages God, she unmasks her Painkiller with more depth and clarity. Through this process she's finding her voice.

Here's her melody line:

Now that wall is beginning to fall. You are allowing me for the first time
to begin to feel again and to live in the reality of my sin. I'm beginning
to understand for the first time the magnitude of what you did on the
cross, you took it, you took it all. I never had to carry any of it.

Just last week she emailed me, "I haven't cut in five days."

So what about you?

If you had to vulnerably cry out to the heavens like Simba or Rose,
what would you say? If you could speak freely and unfiltered, without
any fear of judgment, what would your psalm sound like?

Go ahead and write one. I give you the gift of these four words: I
believe in you.

My Psalm

8

Step Three

Explore Your Wounds

It is impossible for a man to learn what he thinks he already knows.

Epictetus

"What do you want?"

My friend Paul Martinelli asked me this awhile back, and the question ripped through my routine.

He pressed further when I couldn't articulate my desire. "What do you really want?"

I delayed, camping briefly in my uncertainty, but he wouldn't let me go.

"Kary, do you even know what you really want?"

By now you might be able to tell that I hang with some pretty direct people. I even pay money for some of them to coach and mentor me. I want to reach my potential that badly.

But I didn't always invite accountability. Quite honestly, at one point in my life I avoided it altogether. I set up shop in what we call "the comfort zone."

Imagine something big. I mean really, really big.

Overcoming your challenge	Climbing a mountain
Reconciling a relationship	Breaking a record
Achieving your dream	Earning a degree

I don't know what seems out of your reach, but I want you to think about it for a moment. I want you to picture it in graphic detail.

Do you have it? OK, don't lose it.

Now I'll interrupt. Let's think about money. I use money as an example because it's something we can all relate to. We understand the value of a dollar.

Imagine your annual income. If you don't have one, just pick a number.

Now imagine that being your monthly income. Would you like that to be true?

Most people would enjoy such an arrangement. But these same people, if you asked them to sit down with you and create a plan to achieve this, would begin to argue why it's an impossibility.

"You don't understand; I don't have the necessary degree, training, or skills."

"You don't understand; my situation is different."

"You don't understand; I'm from a small town."

"You don't understand; I can't do that."

Simply put, most people argue for what they don't want.

Remember those universal laws we discussed earlier, such as gravity? Time to meet another one, the Law of Argument: *We get what we argue for.*

Most of us say we want more money, but then we'd argue why it can't be a reality for us.

Change the circumstances, and the law still works. Ask a heroin addict if she wants to be free. Odds are she'll say yes. Then, when you try to create a plan, she'll argue why it won't work for her.

"You don't understand; all my friends are heroin addicts too."

"You don't understand; I've never made it a day without it."

"You don't understand; my dealer is my neighbor."

"You don't understand; I need it."

I have a personal policy when I coach people: I never make an agreement with their unbelief. I don't let them off the hook or allow them to hide behind their excuses. This is because I care about them and their potential way too much.

Here's the sad truth: most of us self-sabotage. We don't need to worry about our competition, because we're already set on defeating ourselves. We can even see unbelief in our word choices. When considering our dreams, we quit before we get started. We give ourselves an out.

How much energy will it require?

How much will it cost?

How long will it take?

These phrases already admit defeat and open the door for escape.

Consider a crude example from the life of conquistador Hernando Cortez. Legend has it that before he came to the New World he discussed with his men the potential treasure that resided within the new land. He told them how the treasure could enrich their lives and provide for their children's children.

But when they finally landed on the shore, his men lacked motivation and commitment. They reflected upon those who had made attempts in the past and failed. So Cortez did something unexpected.

He burned their ships.

He eliminated their ability to escape.

He erased their excuses.

Cortez didn't make an agreement with their unbelief.

We might not be exploring new lands today, but most of us are facing a similar challenge. We desire expansion. We want to be more, do more, have more, and give more than we currently experience. But we won't achieve this with *average*.

Nobody wants average, whether it's regarding their food, entertainment, or experience. People pay for excellence. People want exceptional. And although we expect it from others, we often believe it's impossible for ourselves.

We don't get what we want; we get who we are. We're the lid on our own potential and we can never outperform our own self-image.

SO how do we get off the proverbial dime?

Movement starts by first understanding where we stand. Unfortunately, instead of standing in God's truth, too often we stand in the circle of our own truth.

This is the circle of what we believe is possible for us.

This is the circle known as our comfort zone.

This is the circle of our own awareness.

Within this circle we try to convince ourselves that we're content with being content and satisfied with satisfactory.

But we're not.

And when we're not growing and creating the life we know we're meant to experience, our spirit stirs. We use words to describe the place we're at, the place of our discontentment. We conceive something better, but we're not sure how to get there.

We see "stuck" wherever we go. But every so often we let our mind drift to what could be. We daydream, because dreams are free. We fail to realize that dreams are found on a tollway, not a highway. They come with a cost. And unfortunately, we don't pay just once. We pay daily.

Some of us see this cost and crumble. But the price really doesn't matter. The price can be high or low; as long as it's more than we have, we stagger under the weight. We see the gap, take inventory of what we don't have, and become discouraged at the apparent distance we need to travel.

We falter because we think we don't have what it takes, and we sink into a shortage of self-belief. Unfortunately, we don't see value in ourselves and as a result we don't invest in ourselves. Instead, we wait for a sponsor. Even though we lack belief in ourselves, we want others to believe in us.

We fail to understand the Law of Belief: *Before others choose to believe in you, they naturally judge if you believe in yourself.*

We taste our self-limiting beliefs and we sense the void between what is and what could be. This distance is defined as the "gap of intention," or some experts label it as the "intention-behavior gap."[1] In simpler terms, it's the disconnect between knowing and doing.

Morpheus illustrates this gap when he tells Neo, "Stop trying to hit me and hit me!"[2] Although Neo wanted to hit Morpheus, for some reason he couldn't. An obvious gap existed.

In the book of Mark, we see this gap in the dialogue between the father of a demon-possessed boy and Jesus. After Jesus asks him if he's willing to exercise faith, he tells the rabbi, "I do believe, help my unbelief" (9:24 NASB). Although he had faith Jesus could heal people, for some reason he didn't think Jesus could heal his son.

In our own physical health, there are also gaps between our knowing and our doing. We're aware of steps we could take to ensure better physical health, whether it be more exercise, better eating habits, or longer sleeping patterns. But many of us never do these things.

The solution to this gap isn't more knowledge. The gap between knowing and doing is always bridged with being. We're human *beings*, not human *doings*. What we do is always an extension of who we are, not what we know.

But our natural response is fear. We fear our own ability to bridge the gap. We fear failure and exposure. We fear leaving our comfort zone. We suffer from self-judgment and worry what the neighbors will think.

But here's a little secret: the neighbors don't think.

We sit paralyzed with fear about other people's impressions, but they're too caught up in their own story to even care. In our twenties we worry about what everyone thinks of us. In our forties we don't care what people think of us. And in our sixties we realize no one has been thinking of us.

The most critical jury resides inside our own minds, not within other people. And the people around us, the ones we're so afraid of, they're looking to us as an example. They're just as scared, and they're in desperate need of a bold model.

Hence one of the reasons movies are so popular. We enjoy watching other people overcome their own obstacles so we can have courage when facing ours. Unfortunately, we often use the same approach when it comes to our own lives as we do when watching movies. We're spectators in our own lives, accepting our lives rather than leading them.

Although we create a mental model of perfection for our lives, we can't step into it. Although we believe in a better way and a better world, we can't live from it. Although we aspire and long to change, we find ourselves stuck.

And so we do what we were taught to do: we begin to blame. We blame those around us and the circumstances of our life.

We blame our significant other.

We blame our employees.

We blame the economy.

We blame the politicians.

We blame our bosses.

We blame the markets.

And we remain bound to the circumstances and conditions of our lives, never realizing that the content of our lives, our circumstances and conditions, do not need to create a prison.

If we can only get outside ourselves long enough to see the scenery, then we'd acknowledge this other way. To go higher, we must dig Deeper.

Here's what I mean. Look beneath you right now. There's carpet, grass, tile, floor, sand, or air. Now look around you. There are trees, buildings, or walls of some sort. Consider the walls. Have you ever realized what's behind them? Insulation? Drywall? Wood? Nails?

If you're sitting in a chair then consider: Do you feel your back against the chair? Do you feel your feet against the floor? Certainly, there is more than we're aware of. And everything matters. Try to name one thing that doesn't matter.

Consider the little piece of plastic under certain table legs the next time you eat. Think it's unimportant? Try eating your dinner on a wobbly table and you'll quickly thank the designer of that little piece of plastic.

Or try to consider a world without staples the next time you present an important talk. Or one without paperclips, or pens, or personal computers.

I remember putting together one of my kid's Christmas toys one December evening. Toward the end of the project I realized I was missing one small screw. The whole toy fell apart because of an insignificant little part.

Was that screw really insignificant? Are you really insignificant?

IIIII

There are only two types of people and you're either one or the other. There's no third option. The truth is, we live with the mindset of either a victim or a victor. This choice kind of cuts out the middle ground, doesn't it?

So, which "map of the world" do you ascribe to? A victim believes the world happens to them. A victor believes they happen to the world. Either we blame people for our lack, or we take responsibility for what we don't yet possess. Our choice affects the way we see ourselves and the way we see the world around us. It's the vibration we give off to others, and it's the reason we attract some people and repel others. Who we choose to be is who we will become.

I don't know your specific story, but my guess is, like me, you've initiated some Pain during your time on earth. Maybe on the literal playground, or on the playground of life. Compared to what other people have done, the Pain you've dished out might not be much, but if you're breathing then you've contributed to the community. If you've been in relationship with at least one person, even if that person is limited to yourself, then you've bestowed:

Misunderstanding	Violence
Abandonment	Betrayal
Selfishness	Slander
Disrespect	Gossip
Loneliness	Abuse
Bitterness	Theft
Jealousy	

But here's what else I know. You've been on the receiving end too. You've had Pain happen to you, and you've suffered:

Mistreatment	Prejudice
Accusation	Deceit
Unfairness	Blame
Judgment	Greed
Shame	Envy

Guilt   Fear
Hate   Lust

Writing this short Pain list Pains me. I know the hurt I've done to
others and the hurt done to me, and I think of that multiplied by every
reader and it's simply overwhelming. I let all the sins of commission
flood into my awareness and I'm swept away.

But that's not even scratching the surface. What about all the sins
of omission? Think back to all the times we didn't:

Offer a hand to someone in peril
Stand up for someone in trouble
Speak up for someone in need

So here are my questions: How long will we focus on what could
have been, should have been, or might be? How long will we let what's
been done to us in the past define our present?

How long?

Because as long as we dwell on anything but the present then we've
abdicated our divine birthright to have dominion over our day.[3] As long
as we're victims, we're not responsible and we can cling to excuses.
And then it's not our fault, but somebody else's. And then we feel
justified and comfortable and perfectly equipped to blame our lack
on another person or another thing. And in this state the world seems
manageable. Maybe not ideal, but at least predictable and controllable.

When we live from this victim mindset, we find fulfillment in adding to the drama by surrounding ourselves with people who agree
with the story inside our head. We have the same conversations that
strengthen our version of the truth. Our favorite songs confirm the
injustice, and our favorite films add color and richness to our inter-
pretation of correctness.

How long?

I'm not denying your Pain or minimizing your hurt; I'm just asking
a simple question that I'm not equipped to answer.

How long?

What if I showed you that you have more power than you ever
thought or imagined? What if you could peek past your Pain and

into your potential? What if you saw yourself as a victor in every area of your life?

Is that something you'd want? What do you want? What do you really want?

Do you even know what you really want?

9

Step Four

Overcome Your Excuses

He that is good for making excuses is seldom good for
anything else.

Benjamin Franklin

May 5, 1954.

In over six thousand years of recorded history, no man, woman, or
child had ever done the impossible. Up until that day, all of humanity
bought into a particular self-limiting belief—except for a select few.
That's why so many people showed up to see if he could do it. Not
only did the general public believe such a feat was impossible, but
many doctors also weighed in, proclaiming that it was also lethal.

Run a mile in under four minutes and you will die. That's pretty
thick adversity. That's a prediction that could produce some exceptional excuses. Unless, of course, you didn't buy into that self-limiting
belief.

No wonder a crowd showed up at Iffley Road Track in Oxford that
day. They were guaranteed a spectacle, no matter how you sliced it.

Until this time, the best humanity could dish out was a time of 4 minutes and 1.3 seconds, run by Gunder Hagg of Sweden in 1945. A barrier obviously existed, but few recognized it for what it was: a barrier of belief.

Although a psychological mystique hung heavy around the four-minute barrier, several runners in the early 1950s dedicated themselves to being the first to break it. A noble goal; these runners didn't know if they were chasing their death sentence as well. The doctors certainly seemed to think so.

A six-foot-one medical student, Roger Bannister not only believed the impossible was possible, but also that he would be the one to do it. Obstacles were no stranger to Bannister. His parents couldn't afford to send him to school, so he ran his way to admission by winning a track scholarship to Oxford, where he studied medicine and evolved into a running sensation.

Not everything went Roger's way though. He also suffered from self-limiting beliefs at one time. The 1952 Olympics weren't kind to him. After failing dismally with a fourth place finish, Bannister spent two months deciding whether to give up running altogether.

Good thing he didn't.

He intensified his training and did hard interval running with the two-year-old memory of disappointment still burning within him. Although he had failed in the past, each day he trained he took one step closer to his goal. Bannister believed the man who could drive himself further once the effort got Painful would be the man who would win. And so he pushed hard, especially when the Pain set in.

Reporters recorded their observations, and their perspective is just as fresh today as when it was penned over fifty years ago. The AP reported:

> Bannister bided his time until about 300 yards from the tape when he urged himself to a supreme effort. With a machine-like, seemingly effortless stride he drew away steadily from Chataway and, head thrown back slightly, he breasted the cool, stiff wind on the last turn to come driving down the homestretch to climax his spectacular performance.[1]

Although this is an insightful report, Bannister provided us with a better, below the surface, perspective: "No longer conscious of my movement, I discovered a new unity with nature. I had found a new source of power and beauty, a source I never dreamt existed."

He crossed the finish line and collapsed to the ground, drained of energy. "It was only then that real pain overtook me," he said. "I felt like an exploded flashlight with no will to live; I just went on existing in the most passive physical state without being unconscious."[2]

The crowd let loose when the announcer uttered Bannister's time, not even allowing him the privilege of finishing his sentence. All they needed to hear was three minutes and then applause overtook the rest of the announcement: 59.4 seconds.

Looking back now, it's obvious that breaking the four-minute mile was more of a psychological feat than a physical one. Bannister broke a belief first and a record second. Insiders understood that the new record resulted from a new belief. Volumes could be written about the events that transpired shortly after.

Within forty-six days of Bannister's breakthrough, John Landy in Finland surpassed the record with a time of 3:57.9. Many runners followed after.

By the end of 1957, sixteen runners had logged sub-four-minute miles. And in the last fifty years the mile record has been lowered by almost seventeen seconds, an eternity in the running world. Currently, the mile record is held by Morocco's Hicham El Guerrouj, who ran a time of 3:43.13 in Rome in 1999.

Clearly, the four-minute mile barrier resided only in the minds of individuals. Roger Bannister broke that belief, and runners have been breaking the record ever since.

What self-limiting beliefs swim around in your cerebral?
When did you first start believing them?
How do they hold you back?
Where do they surface?
Who planted them?
Why?
Self-limiting beliefs are nothing new. They've been hijacking human hearts and sabotaging human potential since the beginning.

Fear tricks our minds into obeying illogical commands and submitting to unfounded statements. Our subconscious can't easily discern between reality and fantasy. This is why rationalizing with a three-year-old about the pretend monster under the bed doesn't pay big dividends.

We rarely see how self-limiting beliefs prevent potential and hinder healing when it comes to our own lives. Yet if we frame self-limiting beliefs within the backdrop of inventions and technologies, we quickly see the futility and fallacy of such thinking. Thankfully, a few courageous pioneers overcame the excuses that defined the popular thinking of their day. Here are a few famous ones:

> There is no reason anyone would want a computer in their home.
>
> Ken Olson, president, chairman, and founder of Digital
> Equipment Corp. (DEC), maker of big business
> mainframe computers, arguing against the PC, 1977

> So we went to Atari and said, "Hey, we've got this amazing thing, even built with some of your parts, and what do you think about funding us? Or we'll give it to you. We just want to do it. Pay our salary, we'll come work for you." And they said, "No." So then we went to Hewlett-Packard, and they said, "Hey, we don't need you. You haven't got through college yet."
>
> Steve Jobs, founder of Apple Computer, Inc.,
> on his and Steve Wozniak's early attempts
> to distribute their personal computer

> It will be years—not in my time—before a woman will become prime minister.
>
> Margaret Thatcher, future prime minister, October 26, 1969

> With over fifteen types of foreign cars already on sale here, the Japanese auto industry isn't likely to carve out a big share of the market for itself.
>
> *BusinessWeek*, August 2, 1968

> Remote shopping, while entirely feasible, will flop—because women like to get out of the house, like to handle merchandise, like to be able to change their minds.
>
> *Newsweek*, predicting popular holidays for the late 1960s

There is practically no chance communications space satellites will be used to provide better telephone, telegraph, television, or radio service inside the United States.

T. Craven, FCC Commissioner, 1961 (the first commercial communications satellite went into service in 1965)

We don't like their sound, and guitar music is on the way out.

Decca Records, when they rejected The Beatles, 1962

The world potential market for copying machines is 5,000 at most.

IBM, to the eventual founders of Xerox, saying the photocopier had no market large enough to justify production, 1959

To place a man in a multi-stage rocket and project him into the controlling gravitational field of the moon where the passengers can make scientific observations, perhaps land alive, and then return to earth—all that constitutes a wild dream worthy of Jules Verne. I am bold enough to say that such a man-made voyage will never occur regardless of all future advances.

Lee DeForest, American radio pioneer and inventor of the vacuum tube, 1957

Television won't last. It's a flash in the pan.

Mary Somerville, pioneer of radio educational broadcasts, 1948

There is not the slightest indication that nuclear energy will ever be obtainable. It would mean that the atom would have to be shattered at will.

Albert Einstein, 1932

The wireless music box has no imaginable commercial value. Who would pay for a message sent to no one in particular?

Associates of David Sarnoff responding to the latter's call for investment in the radio, 1921

Taking the best left-handed pitcher in baseball and converting him into a right fielder is one of the dumbest things I ever heard.

Tris Speaker, baseball expert, talking about Babe Ruth, 1919

The cinema is little more than a fad. It's canned drama. What audiences really want to see is flesh and blood on the stage.

Charlie Chaplin, actor, producer, director, and studio founder, 1916

The idea that cavalry will be replaced by these iron coaches is absurd. It is little short of treasonous.

> Comment of an aide-de-camp to Field Marshal Haig,
> at tank demonstration, 1916

There will never be a bigger plane built.

> A Boeing engineer, after the first flight
> of the 247, a twin engine plane
> that holds ten people

Sensible and responsible women do not want to vote.

> Grover Cleveland, US president, 1905

Airplanes are interesting toys but of no military value.

> Marechal Ferdinand Foch, professor of strategy, 1904

The horse is here to stay but the automobile is only a novelty—a fad.

> The president of the Michigan Savings Bank
> advising Henry Ford's lawyer, Horace Rackham,
> not to invest in the Ford Motor Co., 1903

Man will not fly for fifty years.

> Wilbur Wright, American
> aviation pioneer, to brother
> Orville, after a disappointing
> flying experiment, 1901
> (their first successful flight
> was in 1903)

I must confess that my imagination refuses to see any sort of submarine doing anything but suffocating its crew and floundering at sea.

> H. G. Wells, British novelist, 1901

It doesn't matter what he does, he will never amount to anything.

> Albert Einstein's teacher to his father, 1895

Fooling around with alternating current is just a waste of time. Nobody will use it, ever.

> Thomas Edison, American inventor, 1889

We are probably nearing the limit of all we can know about astronomy.

> Simon Newcomb, Canadian-born American astronomer, 1888

This "telephone" has too many shortcomings to be seriously considered as a means of communication. The device is inherently of no value to us.

A memo at Western Union, 1878

When the Paris Exhibition [of 1878] closes, electric light will close with it and no more will be heard of it.

Oxford professor Erasmus Wilson

The abdomen, the chest, and the brain will forever be shut from the intrusion of the wise and humane surgeon.

John Eric Ericksen, British surgeon,
appointed Surgeon Extraordinary to Queen Victoria, 1873

No one will pay good money to get from Berlin to Potsdam in one hour when he can ride his horse there in one day for free.

King William I of Prussia, on hearing of the invention of trains, 1864

They couldn't hit an elephant at this dist—

Last words of Gen. John Sedgwick,
spoken as he looked out over the parapet
at enemy lines during the Battle
of Spotsylvania Court House, 1864

Drill for oil? You mean drill into the ground to try and find oil? You're crazy.

Associates of Edwin L. Drake
refusing his suggestion to drill for oil, 1859

The abolishment of pain in surgery is a chimera. It is absurd to go on seeking it . . . knife and pain are two words in surgery that must forever be associated in the consciousness of the patient.

Dr. Alfred Velpeau, French surgeon, 1839

Rail travel at high speed is not possible because passengers, unable to breathe, would die of asphyxia.

Dr. Dionysys Larder, professor of natural philosophy
and astronomy, University College London, 1830

So many centuries after the Creation it is unlikely that anyone could find hitherto unknown lands of any value.

Committee advising King Ferdinand and Queen Isabella of Spain
regarding a proposal by Christopher Columbus, 1486

‗‗‗‗‗

A quick survey reveals that self-limiting beliefs intrude into every facet and fabric of our lives, including:

Entertainment	Literature	Sports
Government	Air travel	Phone
Land travel	Electricity	Music
Technology	Business	Radio
Exploration	Shipping	Film
Astronomy	Medicine	Law
Commerce	Science	War
Computers	Culture	TV
Sea travel	Energy	
Weaponry	Health	

Look around you for a moment.

I just did, and almost everything I see (toys, food, electric light, carpet, shoes, clocks, candy, heating blankets, remotes, reclining furniture, books, cardboard) once encountered self-limiting beliefs.

Everything I see in its current form didn't exist at one time. Humanity needed to overcome the excuses that limited the creation, production, and evolution of such ideas and inventions. Somewhere, sometime, someone felt the need to overcome the excuses. They exchanged popular thinking and conventional wisdom for a higher goal and loftier possibilities. They considered the cost (danger, ridicule, shame) and paid it for something more valuable: potential.

Don't forget, the Wright brothers didn't have a pilot's license. And the laws of flight have always existed. They certainly didn't create them. They simply overcame the excuses and put those laws to work.

So what about you and your context? What self-limiting beliefs are preventing your progress and ensuring your anonymity? What ideas and inventions remain unimagined, undeveloped, and unrefined? What strains of popular thinking and conventional wisdom are restricting you? What about the creation, production, and evolution of your potential?

If you want an excuse, you'll certainly find one. But what happens after you blow through one? Then you blow through another. And another. You will always find more. But do you want your life to consist of exchanging one excuse for another? Sure, there's Pain in stepping out. But there's also Pain in holding back.

I decided long ago to abandon a life of regret. I decided to embrace life, even if it includes failure. Failure means I'm moving. And being stuck stinks.

Maybe, up until this day, you've bought into a particular self-limiting belief. But today this needs to change. Instead of taking inventory of why you can't, begin to reframe your response. Start saying, "Up until now . . . "

Up until now I was enslaved by past failures.

Up until now I let fear hold me back.

Up until now I wouldn't take action.

A barrier obviously exists, but this barrier of belief has sabotaged your success long enough. Although not everything has gone your way, you haven't given up. Like Roger Bannister found out, the people who drive themselves further once the effort gets Painful are the people who will win.

And if you'll push hard, especially when the Pain sets in, reporters will record their observations and skeptics will claim their opinions.

But that's all they are—opinions.

You know the Truth. Because you're fully alive. And receiving healing.

10

Step Five

Embody Your Healing

> You cannot kindle a fire in any other heart until it is burning within your own.
>
> Eleanor Doan

Simon Cowell.

If you found yourself standing in line to audition for a certain talent show a few years back and you heard the name "Simon Cowell," most likely a certain type of feeling swept through your soul.

Fear.

As a talent judge on *American Idol*, Simon Cowell made sure to live up to his infamous reputation. Besides his verbal jabs and no-nonsense style, he'd start the judging process by asking each contestant the same penetrating question.

With a net worth of over 320 million dollars and an annual salary in recent years of 75 million, his one question could be literally categorized as "the million dollar question."[1]

In the height of each season, as he and the other judges observed hundreds of auditions daily, it seems perplexing that he rarely changed his opening question. For some reason, it defined him as much as the brutal insults and honest feedback he so willingly graced us with.

No matter how you feel about Simon, you can't argue with his intuition.

His track record proves he could sniff out superstars like Kelly Clarkson and Carrie Underwood. And his expertise enabled him to identify less than favorable acts as well. He cut through the fog of talent (or lack thereof) and extracted the elite, crowning rock star royalty without a second thought.

All because of one single question.

Before contestants gave their background, said their name, or sang a note, one single question unearthed their confidence, unlatched their tone, and unlocked their story.

One single question.

Do you know what it is, or do you have any guesses?

Not, "What do your friends think of your voice?" or "How long have you been singing?" or "Are you in a band?"

Nope. None of these sufficed.

Instead, the one question Simon asked more than any other was, "What makes you think you're the next American Idol?"

That's it. And the correct answer converted into millions of dollars of revenue. Most contestants gave a variety of replies:

"Because I've won awards for my singing."

"Because I've been doing this all my life."

"Because I have a vocal coach."

But none of these answers caught Simon's attention. Only one answer predicted potential in this multimillionaire's mind. And only one answer will predict your potential.

We've gone pretty Deep thus far, and we're currently at Step Five. We've already addressed the Why of the Deeper Path and most of the How. But we still have one more section to go: the What.

This section will lead us into greater clarity, but before we start we need to explore the dynamics of this Fifth and final Step: Embody Your Healing. Having traveled so far and dug so Deep, it might be tempting to let up a little.

But don't.

Most of the population hangs out at surface level, and few go further than Step One. Regrettably, the Deeper we go, the more people drop out. Few choose Pain and therefore few embody healing.

It's been said that all dreams contain a wishbone, but what they really require is a backbone. Most bail before the payout and quit before the conclusion.

But not you.

You're engaged. You're curious. You're hungry.

Of course you feel fear. We all do. But this is what sets you apart from others. In the words of Cus D'Amato, "The hero and the coward both feel exactly the same fear, only the hero confronts his fear and converts it to fire."[2]

At this last Step we must confront our fears—and in the process we'll find our courage. I've discovered that although I can never silence my fears, I can put them in proper perspective. Instead of letting them occupy the main stage in my life, I've been able to drastically turn down their volume. Now their voices are barely audible, background music at best. Because of this adjustment, I've been able to discover my voice and sing my melody line.

We can only accomplish this by excavating our fears and confronting them one at a time. So get your shovel and let's start digging into the Big Three:

1. Fear of Change
2. Fear of Failure
3. Fear of Success

Here's what they look like.

Fear of Change

Many of us think change is icky because we're creatures of habit. As children we needed change just to survive. If we rejected it we'd still be in diapers, drinking out of baby bottles, and wearing bibs.

As adults we tend to grow out of change fairly quickly. We prefer what we know because it's safer. We stop playing to win and instead we start playing not to lose. We ignore Eric Hoffer's warning: "People will cling to an unsatisfactory way of life rather than change to get something better for fear of getting something worse."[3]

We end up craving routine because we crave control. Giving up control requires a death of sorts. French writer Anatole France said, "All changes, even the most longed for, have their melancholy; for what we leave behind is part of ourselves; we must die to one life before we can enter into another."[4]

No wonder change is scary. To change is to die and then be reborn. This cycle certainly produces growth, but it also produces inevitable Pain. I experience this every time I get a cell phone upgrade. For the first few days I hate my new phone. Even though I know the new technology will help me go further faster, I can't stand the learning curve. But give it three days and I love the new phone and never want to go back . . . until the next upgrade two years later.

Although this is a trivial example, it can be applied to more epic illustrations as well, such as the Law of Sacrifice. John Maxwell coined this Law by explaining, *we need to give up to go up.*[5]

We often misunderstand the Law of Sacrifice and redefine it as the Law of Tradeoff: *exchanging something of lesser value for something of greater value.* Unfortunately, this isn't the truth. Giving up means letting go *first*, without the guarantee of anything in exchange. It's an act of faith that contains a real risk. Charles DuBois referred to it as the ability "at any moment to sacrifice what we are for what we would become."[6]

The Deeper Path contains change at every corner. If we want to walk the Path, then we must be willing to change. But remember, when we change so do our relationships. Truly, many people are addicted to relationships. To continue on the Path we must break free. We can still value relationships as much as anybody else, but we don't derive our worth from them.

Because we're committed to grow and change, we might lose some friendships along the way. But know this: a friend who demands we stay the same isn't a true friend. Synergistic friendships propel us forward, not hold us back. They feel like wind lifting us up, not weights pulling us down.

Eric Hoffer warns us about the cost of not changing: "In times of change learners inherit the earth; while the learned find themselves beautifully equipped to deal with a world that no longer exists."[7]

Life is change. We can either invite it or ignore it. But realize that change will show up at the party with or without an invitation.

Fear of Failure

In my travels as a speaker, I met a man at one of my events who regretfully told me a story from thirty years prior. Evidently, back in high school he sat in class one day with a blank notebook in front of him. The teacher asked him to work out a math problem at the chalkboard. He stood in front of the class for all of three minutes. When he returned to his desk he looked at his notebook, and someone had written FAILURE in capital letters across it.

He told me, "For the next thirty years, that name shaped my life. Every day I ran from the label FAILURE. It held me back and prevented me from taking risks in business and love."

As tragic as this story sounds, I know fear of failure shapes many of us. I think most people believe in reincarnation by the way they live; they're waiting for the next life to come alive.

Bestselling author Rick Warren identifies three types of people: "There are those who make things happen, those who watch things happen & those who have no idea what's happening."[8]

Which one are you? Few of us fall into the first category. We let fear prevent us from even trying.

Others of us suffer from analysis paralysis. We study things to death before stepping into action. John Henry Newman warned, "A man would do nothing if he waited until he could do it so well that no one could find fault."[9]

Truth is, we will fail. It's part of life. But be encouraged: fear means we're moving, growing, and exploring. The alternative is never trying, a clear indication that we're dead.

I've known certain top CEOs and the business cultures they built that demand employees fail a certain amount of the time, as long as they're attempting new things. Failure means employees are expanding beyond their comfort zone.

Theodore Roosevelt, a leader known for risk, adventure, and an entrepreneurial spirit, brought with him a unique perspective on failure:

> It's not the critic who counts, not the one who points out how the strong man stumbled or how the doer of deeds might have done them better. The credit belongs to the man who is actually in the arena; whose face is marred with the sweat and dust and blood; who strives valiantly; who errs and comes up short again and again; who knows the great enthusiasms, the great devotions and spends himself in a worthy cause and who, at best knows the triumph of high achievement and who at worst, if he fails, at least fails while daring greatly so that his place shall never be with those cold and timid souls who know neither victory nor defeat.[10]

Fear of Success

This last fear may sound strange at first, but I see it spring up in my coaching clients more and more. We Deeply fear our own success. And many times it's highly successful people who fear greater success the most.

Here's why.

Success is a type of magnifying glass. The spotlight shines brighter when you're on the platform. Most of us know our flaws and we fear exposure of those weaknesses. We do everything to protect and hide those cracks. We know standing on a bigger stage will guarantee a higher level of scrutiny.

We believe that when we're in the crowd we can at least wear our masks, and that these masks won't shine as bright on stage. We know our makeup can't cover up every imperfection, and so we play small in order to maintain our image. We want a bigger platform—but not one big enough to reveal us.

We fail to understand that success means a Deep awareness of our failures. I find myself sharing my failures more and more. This posture helps me connect with others more easily and it helps me be more believable. The sooner we get comfortable with ourselves, the sooner others will be comfortable around us.

I've been on internationally syndicated television shows sharing the fact that as a pastor I was angry at God and carved cuss words into my body with a knife. Some might be disappointed with me for that reality, but I'm not—because God's not.

And I share my Pain for no other reason than to connect with other people in their Pain. I've found that when I'm authentic, in an appropriate setting, it helps liberate others, allowing them to be more at peace with who they are.

I'm not ashamed of who I am because it's who I am. I don't have to prove myself, because I'm already accepted by the God of the universe.

I love what Catalyst Conference director Brad Lomenick tells young leaders: "People like to feed pigeons, but they also like to shoot at eagles. Leaders, stay focused on your goal amidst criticism!"[11]

If you're going to succeed, you're going to get shot at. But I'll tell you what: there's no feeling like flying. It beats crawling on the ground all hollow.

I know you've probably heard Marianne Williamson's famous quotation. I love it whenever I hear it, because it's so clear. Although I don't agree with her map of the world, I find her words here extremely truthful:

Our deepest fear is not that we are inadequate. Our deepest fear is that we are powerful beyond measure. It is our light, not our darkness that most frightens us. We ask ourselves, Who am I to be brilliant, gorgeous, talented, fabulous? Actually, who are you *not* to be? You are a child of God. Your playing small does not serve the world. There is nothing enlightened about shrinking so that other people won't feel insecure around you. We are all meant to shine, as children do. We were born to make manifest the glory of God that is within us. It's not just in some of us; it's in everyone. And as we let our own light shine, we unconsciously give other people permission to do the same. As we are liberated from our own fear, our presence automatically liberates others.[12]

Just for the sake of comparison, I rewrote this passage from the completely opposite angle. I believe reading it this way will help us get a glimpse of how we often see ourselves. Like I said before, we're often the biggest critic of our own success. But there's nothing redemptive about sabotaging ourselves. Maybe you'll let this next paragraph be the last time you see yourself as anything less than who you've been created to be.

Our Deepest fear is not that we are powerful. Our Deepest fear is that we are inadequate beyond measure. It is our darkness, not our light, that most frightens us. We should ask ourselves, Who am I to be brilliant, gorgeous, talented, fabulous? Actually, you're right, who are you to be? You're not a child of God. Your playing big does not serve the world. There is something enlightening about shrinking so that other people won't feel insecure around you. We are not all meant to shine, as children do. We weren't born to make manifest the glory of God that is within us. In fact, it's only in some of us; not in everyone. And as we let our own darkness shine, we unconsciously give other people permission to do the same. As we are enslaved by our own fear, our presence automatically enslaves others.

See what I mean? This version douses the fire and quenches the passion inside each one of us. And when you're not on fire, neither is your world. Sadly, this is the song many of us keep singing. And this is the way many of us feel and function.

But it's time for us to sing a new song.

It's been said that many people are dead, but they just haven't made it official; the bulk of people die at twenty-five but are buried at seventy-five. I've seen too many real-life examples to think quips like this are funny.

One of my mentors, John C. Maxwell, challenges people to "live until they die." We should accept his challenge and choose to live.

We should embody our healing and play big. Recognize that where our focus goes our energy flows, and so we must feed ourselves not with fear but with faith.

We have to take responsibility for what goes into our own fuel tank. For every fear we meditate upon, we must combat it with ten thoughts of faith. Concentration camp survivor Viktor Frankl, a man who could have let fear consume him, understood the cost of fear: "Fear makes come true that which one is afraid of."[13]

Someone asked me a few years back, "What's the most frequent command in the Bible?" I had to admit I didn't know the correct answer: "Fear not." God told us 366 times, one for every day of the year including Leap Day. He knows and understands our tendencies, and he wants us to break free and embody healing.

So now, at Step Five, are you still afraid? Rest easy; you don't need to fear anything.

Oh, and before we take another step down, do you want to know the correct answer Simon Cowell wanted to hear to his question, "What makes you think you're the next American Idol?"

The answer Simon wanted to hear, the one that predicted potential in his mind, is the same answer we, your tribe, all want to hear from you. It sounds something like this:

Because this is who I was born to be.

Because this is my calling.

Because I already am.

His question served as a window into the contestants' hearts and souls. Simon wanted to see inside. Before he judged their voices, he actually judged their beliefs. Although fear and faith can coexist, one is always stronger. One will always win.

So which one is speaking louder inside of you? Faith or fear?

My advice? Be the part before you get the part. Popular thinking might catch up with you someday, but then again it might not. No worries. When you're this Deep, all the way down to Step Five, those opinions don't matter anymore.

And neither does Simon's.

PART 3

ALIVE

The What

11

One Happy Reunion

This world is a great sculptor's workshop. We are the statues and there is a rumor going round the shop that some of us are some day going to come to life.

C. S. Lewis

There were 155 people, including Captain Sully, hanging in thin air 3,000 feet over New York City.

They found themselves descending rapidly to the earth, without any engine power.

These circumstances are enough to make any pilot wake up in the middle of the night, heart racing, drenched in a cold sweat. But this was the hand life dealt Captain Sullenberger that day. And he had only moments to make his next play.

Thirty seconds after the engines failed, he radioed air traffic control looking for a place to land. LaGuardia and Teterboro were both suggested, but as the plane fell rapidly so did the list of possible options.

Captain Sullenberger informed air traffic control of their inevitable destination: "We're going into the Hudson."

They were two and a half minutes into the flight and just one minute after the bird strike. This decision came with a cost, with passengers and crew watching it unfold, powerless.

One person acted.

I've seen a computer simulation of this infamous flight on You-Tube.[1] Although the flight leaves the viewer in wonderment, what amazes me even more is Captain Sully's cool demeanor and ability to focus in spite of the noise produced by the co-pilot scrambling, the engines failing, the adrenaline pumping, and air traffic control interrupting.

If you listen closely to the dialogue, you'll know what I mean. Perhaps the most important exchange is that between the captain and the co-pilot immediately following the bird strike.

For the first time that day, the captain took control of the plane.

"My aircraft," Sully said.

"Your aircraft," said the first officer.[2]

And with those two words, Sully took responsibility for the situation.

He didn't blame shift.

Or make excuses.

Or complain.

Or stall.

He accepted the challenge even though he never asked for it, realizing this ordeal would define him for the rest of his life. He understood the magnitude of the moment.

His profound explanation to Katie Couric reveals his awareness and carries just as much wisdom as the first time I quoted it in the beginning of this book: "For 42 years, I've been making small, regular deposits in this bank of experience: education and training. And on January 15 the balance was sufficient so that I could make a very large withdrawal."[3]

Sully's poise reflects a certain posture. We also observe this quiet inner confidence in the lives of those who've traveled the Deeper Path.

They accept full responsibility for their lives.

They don't blame shift.

Or make excuses.

Or complain.

Or stall.

They say to those around them, "My life." And then they step up and live into it.

What defines these people is their ability to focus in spite of the noise produced by the masses talking, economies failing, adrenaline pumping, and life interrupting.

This type of focus arises only when something beyond our immediate Pain arises first. Our cross will crush us unless we're able to clearly see our crown that lies beyond. Holocaust survivor Viktor Frankl experienced this reality in a way very few of us will ever understand. Daily his comrades slipped away into the next life. No one would blame them, for they experienced unspeakable Pain.

But Frankl transcended his Pain. He saw past it and into his potential.

I've broken a few of his quotes down into single thoughts so you can let them seep into your awareness, one idea at a time:

Our greatest freedom is the freedom to choose our attitude.

Forces beyond your control can take away everything you possess except one thing, your freedom to choose how you will respond to the situation.

Life is never made unbearable by circumstances, but only by lack of meaning and purpose.

In some ways suffering ceases to be suffering at the moment it finds a meaning, such as the meaning of a sacrifice.[4]

Frankl understood that suffering only makes sense against the backdrop of purpose and meaning.

When we get swallowed up in the moment, we give our power to other people or circumstances. In this space we no longer take responsibility for ourselves but float along as victims dependent upon the whims of forces outside our control. Hopelessness sets in, the unavoidable byproduct of being subject to circumstances.

But neither Frankl nor Sully saw themselves as powerless. They weren't crushed by their circumstances. Instead, they rose above them and exerted control over the only thing they could: themselves. Captain Sully, only seconds away from almost certain death, reflected on his crown and not the cross that confronted him. He told Couric, "My focus at that point was so intensely on the landing. I thought of nothing else." His commitment and confidence never wavered. "It just took some concentration. I was sure I could do it."

And he did just that.

After he landed the plane and the evacuation ended, Captain Sullenberger wanted confirmation. "After bugging people for hours, I finally got the word that it was official. That the count was 155," he recalled.

All survived.

Couric asked Sullenberger what he felt after he heard the news. He said, "I don't remember saying anything. But I remember feeling the most intense feeling of relief that I ever felt in my life. I felt like the weight of the universe had been lifted off my heart."

Clearly, Sully's crown looked like 155 people safe and sound. He saw his crown and then he lived into it.

Weeks later, the crew and passengers were invited to a reunion. When the crew walked into a hotel ballroom in Charlotte, the survivors and some of their relatives gave them a good round of applause.

"Thank you for saving my life," one woman told Sully.

"You just did an incredible job," a man said. "Really, really, really proud."

"More than one woman came up to me and said, 'Thank you for not making me a widow. Thank you for allowing my three-year-old son to have a father,'" Sullenberger said.[5]

On the day of the reunion, he realized something that few of us ever do.

We're all connected.

All 155 people on that plane are connected to everyone else, even to you. If Sully would have failed to take responsibility for the aircraft that day, then thousands and thousands of people would have been affected.

People would have lost their fathers.

Their future grandchildren.

Their future spouses.

Their brothers.

Their sisters.

Their friends.

Life itself would have been altered, forever.

Or even worse yet, imagine if Captain Sully had crashed the plane in densely populated Manhattan with a full tank of fuel. How many lives would have perished, besides those on the plane?

Thankfully, he didn't crash and so they didn't perish.

Don't think your life is any less significant. You have just as much riding on the way you steer your life—maybe even more. Today, you have the opportunity to land safely or crash. And it all depends on your choice to take responsibility for the gift you've been given.

Your life.

꒛꒛꒛꒛

Reunions. Regardless of the type . . .

Grad School	Military
High School	Family
College	

We usually either love or hate them. I haven't met too many people who are neutral about reunions. Growing up, I always enjoyed our family reunions. I can still remember those annual Sunday afternoons in August at a park in Wisconsin.

The pickup games of football.	The games in the lake.
The wide variety of food.	The competition.
The water balloon fights.	The laughs.
The warm introductions.	The fun.

Reunions blend the past, present, and future into one big experience. The past, because we look backward and reminisce. The present, because we explain our current context. The future, because we anticipate what's next.

In good movies and TV shows, reunions often speak to me. I find myself identifying with the characters. I'm drawn in and I begin to feel with them and for them. Compassion, comfort, regret, peace, hope, fear, love, joy—these feelings emerge at different intervals and in different amounts, based on the place each one of us is at. If we've experienced betrayal, then we process the betrayal of a character differently. It's the same thing with loss, luck, or love. Reunions in media evoke a powerful response, because images and stories speak to our subconscious in a way that information doesn't.

Directors and producers often strategically place reunions at some sort of conclusion. Some memorable reunions are captured in *Les Miserables, Tree of Life, The Island, Inception, Gladiator, Tangled,* and *LOST.*

Although I can't claim to be an expert about the television show *LOST,* I caught the last scene of the last episode and was Deeply moved by it.[6]

Do you remember the reunion?

In the final episode, a door opens and we encounter Jack dressed in a nice-looking suit as he is led by his father into a very large room. Classical music, with a variety of stringed instruments, fills the air.

As he walks into the room, he sees many of his friends embracing. Across each of their faces we see smiles, joy, and relief. We feel their genuine and sincere interest in one another as they share in laughter while reminiscing. Each sojourner extends generous and appropriate affection as they reunite after a long spell of separation.

We taste their history together and understand rather quickly that we, the viewers, are experiencing a gathering that is both rare and robust. Collectively, Deep devotion and appreciation for everyone permeates this reunion.

Then the scene changes in a flash, and we observe Jack wounded and wandering through the jungle, looking for a particular spot. With blood-covered hands, disheveled hair, and soiled clothes, he searches intently for something. We feel his desperation but we're not sure what he's looking for. Because of our ignorance, we can't help or provide relevant information. He feels lost and so do we.

These two scenes alternate until eventually we get greater clarity on what's taking place. The attendees at the reunion seat themselves in pews, and it's quite clear they're sitting in a church. Jack and Kate sit hand in hand, Deeply appreciative of the privilege of partaking in this moment together.

Jack's father opens rather large doors at the rear of the church, and immediately a bright light shines throughout the entire room. The attendees now display collective excitement and anticipation. This scene closes with light filling every square inch and we feel contentment, expectancy, and bliss, just like the characters in the story.

Comparatively, in the other scene we understand when Jack finds what he's looking for—a certain space on the jungle floor. He falls to the ground and covers his fatal wound with his hands. After a few seconds a dog joins him on the jungle floor and the camera begins to pan out, giving us a view of Jack from above. After a few seconds we see what Jack sees—a plane low in the sky above him.

As Jack closes his eyes the screen goes black. The title slide *LOST* appears and then fades. As the credits roll, we see water, land, and an apparent plane crash.

Transcending TV for a moment, I must ask: Do reunions resonate with something Deep inside you? If so, it's because you're aware of the Deeper story being written all around us. If we listen closely enough to the rhythms of life, we'll remember that we were meant for reunion. Life is a journey of *return*—back to the One who created us. Returning to our original purpose. Returning to our full potential.

Stripped down to its most basic description, The Deeper Path is reunion.

And a happy one at that.

A goal in this life is to live so fully that we enter the next life empty. Todd Henry, author of *The Accidental Creative*, tells a story about dying empty.

> I was in a meeting in which a South African friend asked, "Do you know what the most valuable land in the world is?" The rest of us were thinking, "Well, probably the diamond mines of Africa, or maybe the oil fields of the middle east?"

"No," our friend replied, "it's the graveyard, because with all of those people are buried unfulfilled dreams, unwritten novels, masterpieces not created, businesses not started, relationships not reconciled. THAT is the most valuable land in the world."

Then a little phrase popped into my head in such a way that it felt almost like a mandate. The phrase was "die empty." While it may sound intimidating, it was actually very freeing because I was suddenly aware that it's not my job to control the path of my career or what impact I may or may not have on the world. My only job—each and every day—is to empty myself, to do my daily work, and to try as much as possible to leave nothing unspoken, uncreated, unwritten.[7]

So what about your life?

Are you pouring out or saving up? Are you waiting or acting? Are you living or dead?

Saint Irenaeus wrote, "The glory of God is a man fully alive."[8] When we're fully alive, we no longer fear death. Feeling peace and not Pain, we no longer fear the sting of an unlived life. Instead, we understand that death simply showcases the destiny we've already discovered.

In the movie *Serendipity* the character Dean, played by Jeremy Piven, said, "You know the Greeks didn't write obituaries. They only asked one question after a man died: 'Did he have passion?'"[9]

What about your life? Do you have passion?

When we choose our Pain rather than avoid it, we come closer to understanding and embracing our passion. We don't need to *write* our obituary just prior to entering the next life. Instead, we *become* it in this life.

The ancients believed our lives were a story known and read by the world. And if we didn't like the way our story read—as long as we still had breath—we could change our story by changing ourselves.

What about your story? Are you content with the way it reads? If not, why not? Let me be the first one to say: you're not too old, too young, too dumb, too smart, too clean, too dirty, too poor, or too rich.

Our greatest work is our own life. And as it is the only thing we can truly control, it's up to each of us to make our greatest contribution. The first step toward changing our story begins by choosing our Pain.

Because you're still breathing, you have the gift of time—and that time is now.

The late Steve Jobs wrote:

> No one wants to die. Even people who want to go to heaven don't want to die to get there. And yet death is the destination we all share. No one has ever escaped it. And that is as it should be, because Death is very likely the single best invention of Life. It is Life's change agent. It clears out the old to make way for the new.[10]

Don't wait until you die before you choose to live. It's too late. And the quality of your reunion depends on it.

The Bible tells us about an amazing reunion that awaits each one of us if we're ready. Let's take a peek at that passage we read earlier. The one about Jesus and the joy he had for his cross. But this time let's look at it through the lens of a reunion.

> Therefore, since we are surrounded by such a great cloud of witnesses, let us throw off everything that hinders and the sin that so easily entangles, and let us run with perseverance the race marked out for us. Let us fix our eyes on Jesus, the author and perfecter of our faith, who for the joy set before him endured the cross, scorning its shame, and sat down at the right hand of the throne of God. (Heb. 12:1–2 NIV 1984)

The author of Hebrews encourages us to focus on Jesus. And so in the next chapter I'd like to give you a glimpse of the Trinity, probably in a way you've never imagined. I believe seeing your Creator will help you create your new life.

Remember, you can only go as high as your view of yourself and your God. And make no mistake, we, your tribe, want you to go as high as you were destined to go. We desire our reunion with you to be full of rejoicing, not full of regret. We believe a happy reunion is possible—and quite simply your purpose.

In the words of Viktor Frankl:

> The crowning experience of all, for the homecoming man, is the wonderful feeling that, after all he has suffered, there is nothing he need fear anymore—except his God.[11]

12

God of Edges

Before God can use a man greatly, he must wound him
Deeply.

Oswald Chambers

I was a first-time dad.

And for the first time, the universe seemed truly at rest.

Holding my new son, Keegan, made letting go of everything else
a simple task. This little guy, whom I had met only a few weeks
prior, now hijacked my head and dominated my thoughts many times
throughout the day and night. Funny how you'd die for someone you
barely know.

The nurse sauntered in bearing a fresh medical chart.

My wife, Kelly, sat in a chair opposite me. She wanted to hold
Keegan, but didn't have the strength. Smart woman—she knew what
was coming.

As a first-time mom, she had probably scavenged the internet the
night before, preparing herself for our little excursion to the doctor's office. I'm sure medical articles and mommy blogs captured the
experience quite accurately.

Lucky for me, I wasn't informed.

Keegan and I cuddled ignorantly over in the corner. I rubbed my cheek up against his little face and he cooed contently without a care in the world. His blue eyes looked up at mine—his tiny pink hand wrapped firmly around my finger. Bundled tightly in his soft blanket, Keegan embodied the definition of safe and secure.

The nurse busily prepared her tray, laying out the sterilized instruments one by one. Although she'd clearly done this many times before, she granted us a moment before graciously interrupting our bonding time.

"Are we ready, Dad?"

Her tone seemed kind but direct—a tough combination to master. Besides, her greeting sounded a bit strange to me. I'd never had a grown woman call me "Dad." Come to think of it, I didn't really enjoy it.

"Yeah," I replied with a twinge of apprehension, unsure of what would happen next.

By answering her question, I took my eyes away from Keegan briefly, just long enough to see her metal tray. What upset me was not the tray itself but rather what was *on* the tray—four plastic syringes poised for Pain. Confronted with the woman in white now armed with needles *longer* than Keegan's arm, my daddy/warrior/protector intuition kicked in.

She inched closer to us, carrying the tray that showcased her weapons of mass destruction. Instinctively, I used my body to box her out, creating space between her and Keegan. He was still cooing—I wasn't about to let some stranger insert four metal spikes into his perfect little frame.

Reading my clear body language, she asked again, this time with a little more intensity, "Are *you* ready, Dad?"

"Umm . . . I guess . . ." I said slowly, letting my aggressive posture slowly fade.

Keegan continued to smile, high on belief and faith in me. In our few short weeks together I had given him no reason to think otherwise. Then a disconcerting thought hit me out of nowhere.

Wanting to prepare Keegan for the Pain he'd soon feel, I thought a word of warning would carry some weight. Maybe even soften the sting. But I realized the kid couldn't talk, or rationalize, or formulate the meaning behind my intended message.

Keegan is going to hate me, my subconscious strongly suggested. *I can see it now . . . these needles are going to wound him for life. Fast-forward fifteen years and he'll be confiding in some counselor about the Pain I put him through—how Daddy tricked him by letting some stranger stick him.*

A pungent smell interrupted my thoughts. Rubbing alcohol. I hated that smell. The smell of anticipation. I knew the agenda coming, but Keegan? He still didn't have a clue. I think he thought the cotton ball saturated with alcohol was meant to tickle his leg.

Holding him closely, I could feel the relaxed pace of his breathing—a stark contrast to my racing heartbeat.

"Dad, I'm going to have to ask you to hold him a little tighter," the nurse said. "He'll want to move around and if he does, it'll make my job harder."

What about my job? Holding down my own son while he suffered from shots? And there it was again, her calling me *Dad.* Her term of endearment—if that's what it was—seemed to have the reverse effect. I began to resent this practitioner of Pain.

Witnessing her hold the first syringe in the air, I braced myself for the inevitable. A second later she thrust the needle into the meaty part of Keegan's leg, emptying the contents almost instantaneously.

Although I wanted to faint, I forced myself to stay alert, Deeply concerned about his reaction. But to my surprise nothing happened.

Or put more correctly, no *sound* happened.

I watched his face rather intently as Keegan seemed to suck up every bit of air that previously inhabited the room. His face quivered and I kept waiting for a noise. Finally, after his lungs had reached their full capacity, he belted out the most shrill, ear-piercing scream I had ever heard.

My heart broke and I wanted to take the next three needles for him—despite my dislike of shots—but I knew I couldn't. Our love for him propelled us to initiate this Pain rather than prevent it. We knew we had to choose this lesser Pain now if we wanted to avoid a greater Pain later.

Still, I took no pleasure at this injustice. I wanted to whisk him away to a place without Pain. Wounding Keegan was killing me, and his cries sunk Deep into my soul. Sensing my apparent alarm, the nurse seemed a tad shaken, but only for a brief moment. She quickly recovered and stuck him with three more syringes. The thought crossed my mind, *Is she trying to kill him?*

Eloquent explanations from Daddy wouldn't work at this age, but even if Keegan could rationalize, what would I tell him?

> Daddy and Mommy love you very much—so much that we're letting this nice lady stick four needles into your body in order to prevent a severe or fatal disease later in life. You see, just like the medical dictionary says, we're "introducing a vaccine, or as some call it, an antigenic substance, into your system as a means to produce or boost your immunity to a specific disease."

Yeah, right.

Pontificating about the purpose of Pain wouldn't alleviate its ache. Sometimes the only thing we can do is to hold the one who's hurting.

And that's exactly what I did—I brought my son close to my chest and kissed the tears that now streaked his face. I knew we were going to push through this newfound Pain that caught us both off guard—the Pain located in his leg and the Pain located in my heart.

⊥⊥⊥⊥

That day with Keegan in the doctor's office I failed to remember one of the central laws of life: with love comes Pain. There's no way around it. And by opening my heart to my newborn baby, I quickly confronted a cost I had not intended to pay.

My inoculation experience—the way a daddy interacts with his child within the context of a Painful situation—is not the view most people have of God and themselves. We can't fathom a heavenly Father who longs to protect us from Pain—a Father who allows Pain in our lives and wishes he could explain its purpose, but realizes we can't always understand.

For some reason, we can't comprehend a kind and loving Father who not only feels our Pain but also desires to take it *from* us by taking it *for* us. Or a Father who realizes that explanations don't eliminate the ache and chooses instead to hold us tightly, look tenderly into our eyes, and kiss the tears from our face.

Sure, part of us wishes that were true, but the other part of us fears letting ourselves believe it. That thought is too Painful, and we reject it because we've been taught to reject Pain. We've been hurt too many times. And besides, we've seen too many impatient and abusive fathers residing on earth to believe that a patient and compassionate God who resides in heaven longs to have a relationship with us.

I've witnessed an interesting trend. Whomever I meet, regardless of their age, gender, industry, preference, economic class, education level, or religious affiliation, I encounter four common misbeliefs about God.

Although not everyone naturally talks about God, if you go a few layers Deep, either personally or corporately, the God subject will surface either directly or indirectly. As much as some of us would like to get away from him, he seems to peek from behind some of life's most common experiences:

A lover's embrace	A gentle breeze
A child's laughter	A spring day
A beautiful song	A sunset

It's like our paths were meant to cross. C. S. Lewis pointed out, "If nothing in this world truly satisfies you, then quite possibly you were made for another world."[1] No wonder we feel homesick for a place we've never been. We might get glimpses of satisfaction in this life, but they're fleeting and infrequent. We feel God's sunshine in the shadows, but we know there's more of him to experience. Augustine addressed this unrealized reality by observing, "Our hearts are restless until they find their rest in thee."[2]

Strangely though, we prefer a distant God or maybe even an angry one. After all, if we abandon God first then he can't abandon us. Those of us who ditch the concept of a loving God—we earn the name *fundamentalists*. And those of us who ditch the concept of God altogether—we're awarded the name *atheists*.

A group of us choose religion. Making God into something he's not proves less hurtful. We try to manipulate and control this false god with good works so we can obtain our most coveted commodity: control. With strict obedience to rules and rituals, we believe our god is somehow appeased and our good behavior will spare us from a Pain-filled existence.

A group of us choose rebellion. Pretending God doesn't exist is less hurtful, and so we make ourselves god. We manipulate people so we can obtain our most coveted commodity: control. With people and possessions in our back pocket, we buy the illusion of a Pain-free existence.

Either way we slice it, we swallow the lie that we're on our own and all alone. We insulate and isolate ourselves from disappointment. And although both paths—rebellion and religion—are dressed up a bit differently, they lead to the same lonely place.

But these strategies and tendencies couldn't be any further off the mark. The truth is that even if we don't believe in God, he believes in us. Despite this reality, we keep trying to outrun him—even us atheists. Unfortunately, we can't seem to get him out of our minds no matter how hard we try.

We write books and prepare speeches about why he doesn't exist. We go to great lengths to explain away his creativity and design, giving credit to random chance instead. We eliminate him from our classrooms and courtrooms—all this effort, just to protect ourselves from Pain. But no matter how hard we try, we can't mask the Pain—or the truth.

The truth doesn't stop us from trying. We feel better by making up stories inside our heads, and usually we settle on one of these four renditions:

1. God isn't aware enough.
2. God isn't strong enough.
3. God isn't present enough.
4. God isn't good enough.

These four misbeliefs arise because we can't wrap our brains around the existence of an all-knowing, all-powerful, all-present good God *and* the existence of Pain. We'd rather reject God altogether than accept a God who allows Pain in our lives. But as much as we'd prefer to live our lives separately from God and then meet up with him in the afterlife, we just keep bumping into him in this life.

Each of these misbeliefs addresses and undermines one of God's attributes. Let's take a look at each one and consider the official term for it, some incorrect assumptions, and the Bible passage that confronts it.

1. God Isn't Aware Enough

God can't be omniscient (all-knowing). God might know about the big things in life before they happen, like who's going to be the next president or pope, but he certainly doesn't know what's coming next for us. If he knew about any future Pain that awaited us, of course he'd protect us from it. Wouldn't he?

> You have searched me, LORD,
>   and you know me.
> You know when I sit and when I rise;
>   you perceive my thoughts from afar.
> You discern my going out and my lying down;
>   you are familiar with all my ways.
> Before a word is on my tongue
>   you, LORD, know it completely. (Ps. 139:1–4)

2. God Isn't Strong Enough

God can't be omnipotent (all-powerful). God might be able to stop the sun or calm the storm, but he can't control the situations in our lives. If he saw us in Pain, of course he'd save us. Wouldn't he?

> I am the LORD, the God of all mankind. Is anything too hard for me? (Jer. 32:27)

3. God Isn't Present Enough

God can't be omnipresent (all-present). God might fill the vast galaxies and the microscopic cellular structures, but he remains clearly absent from our circumstances. If God was with us and if he felt our Pain, he'd stop it from hurting us. Wouldn't he?

> Where can I go from your Spirit?
>   Where can I flee from your presence?
> If I go up to the heavens, you are there;
>   if I make my bed in the depths, you are there.
> If I rise on the wings of the dawn,
>   if I settle on the far side of the sea,
> even there your hand will guide me,
>   your right hand will hold me fast.
> If I say, "Surely the darkness will hide me
>   and the light become night around me,"
> even the darkness will not be dark to you;
>   the night will shine like the day,
>   for darkness is as light to you. (Ps. 139:7–12)

4. God Isn't Good Enough

God can't be omnibenevolent (all-good). God might bestow his graciousness and goodness upon his favorite people, but he withholds his generous hand from us. If God was good, he'd take away anything that would inconvenience us. Wouldn't he?

> He who did not spare his own Son, but gave him up for us all—how will he not also, along with him, graciously give us all things? (Rom. 8:32)

What if the answer to these four questions is no? What if God doesn't:

Protect us from the Pain
Save us from the Pain
Stop the Pain
Take the Pain

Would he still be good, and would he still be God?

These questions do matter. A book that addresses Pain and our potential in that Pain can't sidestep the God question.

Most of us assume that God always gets what God wants. He's God, right? But what if God doesn't always get what he wants?

Did he want the loyal guy who clocked thirty years in the company to get fired? Did he want the child to suffer from lack of food last night? Did he want the innocent woman to get raped? Did he want his Son to die on the cross?

Are we sure God always gets what God wants? Or are we both—God and us—caught between two ideals and sandwiched between two systems? Maybe that's why all creation cries out, awaiting its redemption.

> The creation itself will be liberated from its bondage to decay and brought into the freedom and glory of the children of God. We know that the whole creation has been groaning as in the pains of childbirth right up to the present time. (Rom. 8:21–22)

Maybe God is just as eager for the time when sin, death, and Pain will be eradicated for good. "He will wipe every tear from their eyes. There will be no more death or mourning or crying or pain, for the old order of things has passed away" (Rev. 21:4).

Although Pain will eventually be eradicated, this side of eternity Pain does have its place. The question is, do you trust God? I don't know what unspeakable Pain you've caused and I don't know what type of unspeakable Pain you've had done to you. But here is what I do know:

God was there with you when it happened.

God could have stopped it.

God knew it was coming.

And God is still good.

Those thoughts might not comfort you in the slightest. Actually, they might make you even angrier. But like I said in the beginning, all I am offering you is the truth. I know you want to hear the truth, not some sugarcoated, greeting-card rendition of life. If it makes you upset, then tell God. He can handle it.

Who else can we lean on, depend on, or rely on? Ourselves?

Write another psalm to God and pour out your Pain. Push into him. Feel Deeply. Choose your Pain rather than run from it.

I can't easily explain how Pain and an all-knowing, all-present, all-powerful, and all-good God can coexist. A number of people have tried. They've engaged in theological gymnastics and created constructs such as Open Theism in order to make the struggle easier to swallow. But I'd rather not insult your intelligence. I respect you enough to lay it all out, even if we can't reconcile the paradox.

This issue will always have unknown edges, and so we have a choice. We can either create a new, smooth god in our own image or we can let the God of edges smooth out our rough edges.

Your choice.

"You see, we are like blocks of stone out of which the sculptor carves forms of men. The blows of his chisel, which hurt so much, are what makes us perfect."[3]

13

Soul on Fire

Set yourself on fire and people will come for miles to watch you burn.

John Wesley

"What's the most powerful weapon on earth?" Chet asked me casually over coffee at Panera one Friday morning.

"I don't know, man," I answered. "And you're killing me with these questions," I teased back.

Chet and I have a good relationship where we can jest. But sometimes his questions provoke a bit of frustration. You see, he never reveals the answers but always makes people figure it out for themselves.

"I don't know . . . the atom bomb?" I said, guessing.

"Nope," Chet replied.

"Come on. Give me the answer," I pleaded. "OK . . . love," I tried one more time.

"Nope."

Chet enjoyed this torture way too much.

"Trust me. I'm not going to get this one," I petitioned sincerely.

Maybe he was having an off day, because Chet surprisingly gave me the answer.

"The most powerful weapon on earth is the human soul on fire."
Enjoying that particular melody line, I curiously asked, "Who said that?"

On a roll, Chet replied, "Ferdinand Foch."

And for the next hour of our session Chet and I explored the nooks and crannies of that single thought.

I have to agree with Ferdinand; the most powerful weapon on earth is the human soul on fire.

Fast-forward several years, and I've worked and reworked that quote a thousand times over. Today, I believe that truth so Deeply that I've integrated it into everything I do. It's now my motto: Igniting Souls.

Even though you might not agree with a Soul on Fire, you can't ignore one. We observe this quality in the people who have shaped our world the most, people like Martin Luther King Jr., William Wilberforce, Abraham Lincoln, Nelson Mandela, Mother Teresa, Gandhi, and Jesus.

Although there are many more examples in history, every Soul on Fire knew what they believed and what they valued. They knew who they were and what they loved. They might not have understood exactly how they were going to fulfill their purpose, but that didn't matter. Because they had clearly answered their "why," their "how" was bound to happen sooner or later. I've observed that people who've lost their way are people who've lost their why.[1]

German philosopher Friedrich Nietzsche observed, "He who has a why to live can bear almost any how."[2] Souls on Fire know their why, and they ignite everyone and everything they come in contact with. Interacting with them demands a response, because they're not lukewarm. This doesn't mean that everyone will accept or enjoy them, and many don't. But these folks never need other people's permission to be on fire anyway.

Critics and skeptics will always weigh in with their "why nots." And unless our "why" is bigger than these "why nots," we'll stop before we start. We must decide ahead of time what we want.

I've discovered that a major key in *getting* what we want is *knowing* what we want.

Jesus often asked a question along these lines when interacting with people, especially sick people. At times, the all-knowing Son of God seemed cruel when asking the penetrating, sometimes obvious question, "What do you want?" But Jesus never seemed satisfied with shallow conversations. He wanted to dig Deeper and get below the surface. Like the time he met the man who'd been sick for thirty-eight years.

> Some time later, Jesus went up to Jerusalem for one of the Jewish festivals. Now there is in Jerusalem near the Sheep Gate a pool, which in Aramaic is called Bethesda and which is surrounded by five covered colonnades. Here a great number of disabled people used to lie—the blind, the lame, the paralyzed. One who was there had been an invalid for thirty-eight years.
>
> When Jesus saw him lying there and learned that he had been in this condition for a long time, he asked him, "Do you want to get well?" (John 5:1–6)

What was Jesus thinking? Wasn't it obvious? Of course the lame man wanted to get healed.

Why wouldn't he want that?

We would do well to ask ourselves why we don't want to be healed sometimes. Notice the man never answered Jesus's question. He simply told his story. He explained his cross in detail without even considering the crown offered to him at that very moment.

> "Sir," the invalid replied, "I have no one to help me into the pool when the water is stirred. While I am trying to get in, someone else goes down ahead of me." (v. 7)

In this particular situation Jesus didn't even entertain his excuses. He simply cut through the noise and healed him.

> Then Jesus said to him, "Get up! Pick up your mat and walk." At once the man was cured; he picked up his mat and walked. (vv. 8–9)

We find Jesus's question buried other places in the Gospels. In the story of Bartimaeus we hear a different song, but the same melody line. Jesus confronted him with the same penetrating question: "What do you want?"

Then they came to Jericho. As Jesus and his disciples, together with a large crowd, were leaving the city, a blind man, Bartimaeus (which means "son of Timaeus"), was sitting by the roadside begging. When he heard that it was Jesus of Nazareth, he began to shout, "Jesus, Son of David, have mercy on me!"

Many rebuked him and told him to be quiet, but he shouted all the more, "Son of David, have mercy on me!"

Jesus stopped and said, "Call him."

So they called to the blind man, "Cheer up! On your feet! He's calling you." Throwing his cloak aside, he jumped to his feet and came to Jesus.

"What do you want me to do for you?" Jesus asked him. (Mark 10:46–51)

Bartimaeus was different from the lame man sitting at the pool. He's the one who engaged Jesus, and it's clear what he wanted.

But in the other story, it's Jesus who engaged the lame man at the pool. It's unclear what he wanted.

Two stories. Two sick men.

One question. Two answers.

One excuse. One request.

The blind man said, "Rabbi, I want to see." (v. 51)

Bartimaeus knew what he wanted and he got what he wanted; Jesus honored his request because of his faith.

"Go," said Jesus, "your faith has healed you." Immediately he received his sight and followed Jesus along the road. (v. 52)

But the lame man didn't know what he wanted. He got something he may or may not have wanted. You and I both know there are plenty of people who would rather remain sick and stuck in the familiar than be healed and free in the unfamiliar.

So with your permission, may I ask: What do you want? Do you desire to be healed and free in the unfamiliar?

Are you thinking more about your excuse or your request? Are you focused more on your cross or your crown? Isn't it about time to clarify your crown? What's your decision?

I've learned why some of us struggle so much when making decisions. Maybe this is why the lame man struggled with Jesus's question. And maybe this is why some of us are struggling right now.

"Why?" you might ask.

Humor me for a moment with a quick lesson in Latin. The etymology of the English word *decide* comes from the Latin word *decidere*, which means "to cut off." And its cousin, the related Latin word *caedere*, means "to cut" or "to kill."

Our English word *homicide* comes from this same Latin word *caedere*. So when we make a decision, we are literally "killing our options." We are cutting off the chance to remain open to other possibilities. In a strange way, whenever we make a decision we experience a type of loss.

And so many of us avoid making decisions because we think we're preventing ourselves from feeling loss. However, what we fail to realize is that *not* making a decision is actually a decision in and of itself. We will never be confronted with that exact same opportunity in that exact moment ever again. By choosing not to decide, we are actually choosing to stay exactly where we are.

Dan Ariely, author of *Predictably Irrational*, explains the psychology behind indecision. "Closing a door on an option is experienced as a loss, and people are willing to pay a price to avoid the emotion of a loss."[3]

There is a cost in deciding, but there is also a cost in not deciding. The last chapter is completely up to you. It's your decision if you want to continue.

This is probably not a surprise to you, but we're going to go even Deeper. We'll move from spectator to participant, from reader to leader. We'll define our own destiny and author our own OPUS.

So grab a matchstick and get ready to burn brightly. That is, if you want to become a soul on fire.

14

Author Your OPUS

> We are half-hearted creatures, fooling about with drink
> and sex and ambition when infinite joy is offered us, like
> an ignorant child who wants to go on making mud pies
> in a slum because he cannot imagine what is meant by the
> offer of a holiday at the sea. We are far too easily pleased.
>
> C. S. Lewis

We have a certain room in our house with a rather odd name. I'm not sure who named it, probably my wife, Kelly, but now even our three kids refer to it by this strange name.

We call it the Scary Room.

It's obvious why we gave it this name; the room is inhabited by some yucky types of bugs. Any time we go into the Scary Room and pull out a storage item—whether suitcases or toys—inevitably we find a stowaway spider or sneaky centipede clinging to our contents. We call it the Scary Room because certain people in our household are afraid to go into it.

But I've recently changed the name of the room after reading an email from my friend Dr. Kevin Doherty, who serves as an emergency room physician. After reading a blog post I wrote on fear, he sent me some of his thoughts that originated out of his experience as a medical professional. With his permission, I've included his email below to help inspire some courage within us all.

It is interesting how without fear one could never be courageous. By definition courage is to overcome fear.

It is like the body's immune system. When working properly it requires an exposure to an antigen before it can develop an antibody. If we never expose ourselves (i.e., The Bubble Boy) we will always have an immature immune system.

Some studies report an infant will develop 12–17 viral upper respiratory infections in the first 12 months. That is normal and they just have to run their course. Try telling that to a parent who is up all night with a child that cannot breathe through their nose, cough, congestion, muscle aches, fever. . . . Mom, Dad, child, everybody becomes miserable. It is only normal for a parent to want the magic bullet medicine to make it all go away. Sure, some of these viral infections will develop into secondary bacterial infection due to stagnant mucous/fluid in a nice warm environment (98.6 deg.), like pneumonia, otitis media, sinusitis.

With my older children I think back how many times, out of not wanting them to suffer, I prevented them from the experience of fear, when really I just stole their possibility of overcoming and being courageous. With the clarity of hindsight every well-intending parent could make a list of exposures thwarted by their overprotective fear. In doing so we unintentionally transfer our fear to our child by preventing their ability to develop antibodies. Not only physiologically but spiritually, emotionally, socially, recreationally.

After reading Dr. Doherty's thoughts I had to change the name of the Scary Room. I didn't realize that I was robbing my children of the ability to become courageous. Plus, I didn't like that I was communicating to my kids that they were growing up in a house with a Scary Room. Who wants to think back on their childhood with that stigma?

And so I've renamed it the Courage Room. I now see it as a space of opportunity, a space where we can overcome our fears instead of feel conquered by them.

Don't call children's protective services on me too quickly. I'm not planning on throwing the kids into the newly named Courage Room in order to toughen them up. If they choose to steer clear of the room out of fear, that's up to them. I just don't want to be the one fostering the fear any longer.

Most of us have a Scary Room somewhere in our hearts. We have a certain door we don't want to open because we're afraid of what we might find. But as long as we avoid that room, then we're not truly free. We need to reconsider that room, and instead of seeing it as the Scary Room we need to see it as the Courage Room. If we're willing to explore that room, then it becomes a space for opportunity rather than a space for obstacles. And so I'm inviting you into that Scary Room located within your heart. Once inside, I'm asking you to rename it with a certain Latin word you might not be very familiar with.

Minus the words we discussed in the last chapter, my Latin skills are a bit lacking. I know only two other Latin words, *labōr* and *opus*. And because of its meaning, thanks to my builder, Chet Scott, one of these words (*opus*) has secured a spot on the list of my top ten favorite words of all time. That's a big deal for an author, someone who finds Deep meaning in words.

Here's the definition of each Latin word:

1. *Labōr*: toil, work
2. *Opus*: masterpiece, work

Although these words seem similar on the surface, when we dig Deeper we find out they're actually miles apart.

Although the Deeper Path leads us through our Pain, the OPUS process leads us straight into our potential. And buying into our OPUS means buying into the belief that our lives can and should be our greatest work—our masterpiece.

Once we understand the OPUS process, we have the opportunity to author our own. Authoring my OPUS has helped me clarify who I am and what I should do. This process took time and effort and, most importantly, a builder who was willing to push me Deep—Deep past my barriers of belief.

I'm incredibly indebted to my builder, Chet, and his transformational work that flows from the company he founded, Built to Lead. Our relationship began in 2001, and he's Deeply influenced me. In this chapter I'll share part of the process he created. If you would like to get the full scope of his work, I encourage you to check out his website.[1] My hope is that this process helps provide you with greater clarity as you journey through your Pain and into your potential.

If you're ready to enter that room and author your own future, then let's begin. We'll start by examining a peculiar quotation from a relatively unknown author named L. P. Jacks penned nearly a hundred years ago. Let the weight of his words sink slowly into your awareness.

> A master in the art of living draws no sharp distinction between his work and his play; his labor and his leisure; his mind and his body; his education and his recreation. He hardly knows which is which. He simply pursues his vision of excellence through whatever he is doing, and leaves others to determine whether he is working or playing.
> To himself, he always appears to be doing both.[2]

I remember the first time I read that. Something inside me jolted free—a part that had been asleep for quite a long time. I thought, *I want that to be my reality.*

How can someone argue with truth? We enjoy the option of ignoring truth or embracing it. But we accomplish nothing by arguing with it.

Regrettably, the majority of people don't experience OPUS regarding their work. They only experience the definition of *labōr*. To them, work is a necessary evil, and that's why they call it *work*, right?

Not so fast.

Work was never meant to be the problem. Maybe our perspective of it is—our disengagement while in it and our attitude while at it. Over a decade ago, the Gallup organization discovered some shocking statistics about engagement in the workplace. Here are the brutal findings:

16 percent of the US working population is actively disengaged.

55 percent of the US working population is not engaged.

29 percent of the US working population is engaged.[3]

When a person is disengaged at work, then he or she is toiling. There's no other way of understanding it. Work ceases to be a labor of love but only becomes a job, a burden, a task.

Disengagement from our jobs comes with a fairly hefty price tag. In the past, conservative estimates have come in between $292 billion and $355 billion a year within the US economy alone.

But there are emotional costs as well.[4]

Swiss psychiatrist Carl Jung said, "The greatest burden a child must bear is the unlived life of the parent."

When disengaged parents or guardians come in from a long day at work and their first response is to "kick the dog" out of frustration, they're kicking much more than the dog.[5] They're kicking their children's hope and optimism about their own future. Children take cues from what they see. They watch closely and listen intently. If their parents or guardians feel trapped, enslaved, or angry about their jobs, then what hope do they have when considering their own future?

Their undeveloped minds struggle to understand the logic of staying in school only to eventually enter a job they're going to hate. Why exert energy if frustration is all they have to look forward to?

But thankfully, there's another option besides *labōr*.

OPUS.

Before we dig into OPUS, we first need to break down the three Gallup categories.

One: 16 percent of the US working population is actively disengaged. "Actively disengaged" is a powerful, offensive posture. Remember, it's proactive. This refers to people who are taking action in order to communicate their disengagement. Think measurable, calculated, strategic attempts to display how they feel. We see their disengagement by their behavior:

Stealing from their department	Planting disunity
Sabotaging co-workers	Spreading lies
Hijacking meetings	

These types of people aren't just in the wrong seat on the bus.[6] They intend to steer the bus *off* the cliff. As a fellow passenger, this can make you a little nervous, can't it?

Two: 55 percent of the US working population is not engaged at work. "Not engaged" might rank better than "actively disengaged," but it's still not enough. When more than half of a team couldn't care less about their work, then the organizational culture isn't healthy. At this level employees' efforts are lacking energy; remember, they're unengaged.

They do just enough to get by. And when you only "get by," then soon you'll go *bye-bye*. That is, if your boss cares enough to notice. But often he or she isn't engaged either. And when you have an organization comprised of 71 percent of people who are either actively disengaged or unengaged, then odds are that your organization is experiencing *labōr*, not OPUS.

Unengaged employees tell unsatisfied customers, "Hey, don't ask me, I just work here." These players would rather not have their names on their jerseys. They enjoy their anonymity because they're not proud of their company or their role on the team. They're mercenaries, highly or poorly paid laborers, who flee at the first sign of trouble.

Three: 29 percent of the US working population is engaged. Less than three out of ten people are engaged in their jobs. This minority takes responsibility and ownership of the details. They realize their work is an extension of themselves, and because they're on fire, so is everything they touch.

No one needs to wake up an engaged person. They're living the dream. And don't try taking their dream away from them. You can't, because it's embedded in who they are. As Charles Hedges accurately observed, "A dream is not something that you wake up from, but something that wakes you up."[7]

Engaged people wake up ready to embody their OPUS. They realized long ago that their lives are getting the exact results they're designed to get. If they were ever disengaged in the past, then they stopped complaining and started changing themselves. They found within themselves the ability to choose their attitude and reflect Albert Camus's reality: "In the middle of winter I at last discovered that there was in me an invincible summer."[8]

Tragically, most of us are spectators within our own lives. We embody passivity and we simply accept our lives rather than lead them. This posture produces stress and frustration. Henry David Thoreau addressed this phenomenon, observing, "The mass of men lead lives of quiet desperation."[9] Oliver Wendell Holmes concluded the lament by reflecting, "Alas for those that never sing, but die with all their music in them."[10]

Misdirected living naturally invites noise because we don't know where we're going. We're addicted to other people's voices because we've forgotten what our own voice sounds like.

The exchange in Lewis Carroll's *Alice's Adventures in Wonderland* between Alice and the Cheshire Cat rings true. Confronted with a fork in the road, Alice asks the Cat which road she should take. In a common paraphrase of the dialogue, the Cat replies, "If you don't know where you are going, any road will get you there."[11]

Truly, life brings forks in the road at every turn, and if we haven't authored our OPUS then each decision is an agonizing, drawn-out experience of mysteriously evaluating the pros and cons. Because we don't have a GPS for our dreams, we roll the dice and hope for the best.

But what is *best*? And how would we even know if we had *best*?

Those of us who have traveled The Deeper Path and authored our OPUS already have a clear picture of what's best. Our thinking has already been done because we know what we want. We've invested the difficult time clarifying what we should say yes to, and so now we know what we should say no to.

Authoring our OPUS is a process that helps us become the driver of our destiny and the captain of our calling. Although our steps are ordained by our Creator, he invites us to co-create with him.

Our OPUS embodies the potential on the other side of our Pain, and the crown beyond our cross. We observe it within Bono's melody line, Jesus's passion, Sully's landing, and Gabby's voice.

OPUS, an acrostic developed by Chet Scott of Built to Lead, packs a colossal punch and is a great weapon to ward off disengagement. Understanding the OPUS process will open our eyes, but authoring our OPUS will give us vision. This slight distinction yields huge dividends.

Let's start digging into it.

Explaining OPUS

OPUS is simple to understand but rich in application. Here's a quick breakdown:

O = Overarching Vision
P = Purpose
U = Unifying Strategies
S = Scorecard for Significance[12]

Overarching Vision

This is your Big Dream for your work. Remember Martin Luther King Jr.'s "I have a dream" speech? Notice he didn't say, "I have a plan." Rather, he spoke in pictures that lodged Deep into the hearts and minds of his listeners. When you write yours (about a paragraph long), don't worry about other people's opinions. Discover your own melody line.

> Don't ask yourself what the world needs. Ask yourself what makes you come alive, because the world needs people who have come alive.
> Howard Thurman

> Dream no small dreams for they have no power to move the hearts of men.
> Goethe

Purpose

This is the defining statement of your work. Most artists autograph their masterpieces, but surprisingly, art critics don't need to read the name of the artist in order to discover who created it. They know his or her identity simply based on the subtle nuances of shade, technique, color choice, style, and medium of the artwork. Likewise, the defining statement of your work should be so distinguishable that people who observe your work are able to attribute it back to you. Your purpose (one sentence) is the way you sign your work.

> Every job is a self-portrait of the person who did it. Autograph your work with excellence.
> Unknown

Never give up on something that you can't go a day without thinking about.

Unknown

Unifying Strategies

These are the big buckets of productive actions necessary for you to achieve your Overarching Vision. Most people have too many strategies in theory but never implement them in reality. Brilliance is discovered in simplifying and genius in decluttering. Your unifying strategies (aim for three to five, not thirty-five) keep you focused and on the right path to make sure you arrive at your Big Dream.

A designer knows he has achieved perfection not when there is nothing left to add, but when there is nothing left to take away.

Antonie de Saint-Exupery

Genius is the ability to reduce the complicated to the simple.

C.W. Ceran

The ability to simplify means to eliminate the unnecessary so that the necessary may speak.

. Hans Hofmann

Scorecard for Significance

This is how you know you're hitting your target. Think in terms of baby steps to your Big Dream. If Unifying Strategies are understood as buckets, then your Scorecard for Significance can be thought of as the content within those buckets. Think metrics, but much Deeper than surface topics like revenue or profit. Your scorecard is a compilation of the specific milestones unique to each Unifying Strategy. (Aim for identifying three to five milestones for each strategy.)

Nothing . . . proves a man's ability to lead others, as what he does from day to day to lead himself.

Thomas J. Watson

He who looks outside, dreams; who looks inside, awakes.

Carl Jung

All human beings are alike in seeking happiness. Where they differ is in the objects from which they seek it and the strength they have to reach the objects they desire.

Os Guinness

Exploring OPUS

At this point your OPUS might seem a bit fuzzy. That's OK. Some of the vocabulary can sound strange because most of us haven't ventured into our Scary Room before. Honestly, very few of us have an accurate handle on our Big Dream or purpose because these aren't topics we explore every day.

Before I invite you to author your OPUS, a little detour might help. Sometimes we need to go backward before taking such a huge leap forward. Remember our conversation about good Pain and bad Pain, and the statistics about chronic back Pain (see chap. 4)?

If not, here's a little refresher.

Chronic back Pain is an epidemic in many parts of the world, including America. According to the American Chiropractic Association, 31 million Americans, or around 10 percent of the population, experience lower back Pain at any given time. Half of all working Americans admit to having chronic back Pain symptoms each year. Back Pain is one of the most common reasons for missed work. Experts estimate that as much as 80 percent of the population will experience a back problem at some time in their lives.[13] And the alarming statistics go on and on.

You might wonder what back Pain has to do with authoring our OPUS. In a word—everything.

Remember, research reveals that "weak or poorly controlled core muscles have been associated with low-back pain."[14] One strategy for overcoming chronic back Pain is to develop a stronger core. Our core is made up of a group of muscles we refer to as our "six pack." Also known as the rectus abdominis, the six pack is a paired muscle that runs vertically on each side of the anterior wall of the abdomen. The condition of these core muscles Deeply affects our overall physical health.

However, this illustration of a strong core seeps into other areas of our life too, such as the ability to implement our OPUS. If we lack a strong CORE we're unable to live out our OPUS.

A strong CORE comes by clarifying and then strengthening our Six Pack. Maybe you didn't even know you had a Six Pack, but everyone does—knowingly or unknowingly. It's the operating system behind everything we do. Unfortunately, not everyone has a strong one. This requires time, energy, and Pain. Here's a breakdown of our CORE, reflected by our Six Pack:

The CORE Six Pack

1. Worldview
2. Identity
3. Principles
4. Passion
5. Purpose
6. Process

After we explore the CORE Six Pack, I encourage you to author your own OPUS and clarify your own Six Pack. This process will help you go even further down The Deeper Path and into your potential.

1. WORLDVIEW—WHAT I BELIEVE

This is how you see the world. Start each sentence with "I believe" statements.

> I believe one writes because one has to create a world in which one can live.
>
> Anais Nin

2. IDENTITY—WHO I AM

This is how you see yourself. Start each sentence with "I am" statements.

> Until you make peace with who you are you will never be content with what you got.
>
> Doris Mortman

3. Principles—What I Value

This is what defines worth in your life. Start each sentence with "I value" statements.

It's not hard to make decisions when you know what your values are.
Roy Disney

4. Passion—What I Love

This is who or what you cherish. Start each sentence with "I love" statements.

People living Deeply have no fear of death.
Anais Nin

5. Purpose—Why I Live and Work

This is your "why." Start each sentence with "I help" statements that explain why you live and work.

The glory of God is man fully alive.
Saint Irenaeus

6. Process—How I Will Do It

This will become your Playbook of Productive Action (or POP). We need our OPUS to POP off the page and into our lives. After you author your OPUS and clarify your Six Pack then you can integrate it with your calendar. Beginning with today, look one month out and organize your next four weeks based around your Unifying Strategies. Each month should contain all of your Unifying Strategies and specific relevant action steps defined in your Scorecard for Significance.[15]

Yesterday is ashes; tomorrow wood. Only today does the fire burn brightly.
Eskimo proverb

This type of writing takes time. It's Painful, because strengthening our Six Pack doesn't come easily. Just like developing a physical six pack takes intense effort, so does developing a personal one.

In a physical sense, introducing acute Pain in the form of core muscle exercises (push-ups, sit-ups, planking, and so forth) can help eliminate chronic back Pain. By choosing acute Pain, we allow our hurts the power to heal us. Likewise, in a holistic sense, introducing acute Pain in the form of writing and coaching exercises about our CORE can help us overcome chronic life Pain. And similarly, by choosing acute Pain we give our hurts the power to heal us.

Your CORE Six Pack

So are you ready to clarify and strengthen your Six Pack? Before we can build "the great work out there" (our OPUS), we must first build "the great work in here" (our Six Pack). And although Socrates exhorted us to "know thyself," many of us are strangers in our own skin.

It's time to meet yourself. So find a quiet space and start writing.

1. Worldview—What I Believe
   I believe . . .

   _____

   _____

   _____

2. Identity—Who I Am
   I am . . .

   _____

   _____

   _____

3. Principles—What I Value
   I value . . .

   _____

   _____

   _____

4. Passion—What I Love
   I love . . .

   _____

   _____

   _____

5. Purpose—Why I Live and Work
   I help . . .

   _____

   _____

   _____

6. Process—How I Will Do It
   Revisit this section once you author your OPUS . . .

   _____

   _____

   _____

Most people have to rewrite their CORE Six Pack a number of times. Don't be discouraged. This process, which takes time and energy, becomes the GPS for your dreams. After you clarify your CORE, then take a stab at authoring your OPUS.

Your OPUS

I've found that most Big Dreams include three elements: someone, something, and somewhere. Or put another way: a tribe, a cause, and a space.

According to author Seth Godin in his book *Tribes*, a tribe is "a group of people connected to one another, connected to a leader, and connected to an idea."[16] Your tribe is the people who matter to you.

A cause could be a movement, a product, or a service. It's the idea that you rally around.

A space could be literal or metaphorical. It might reflect the physical space your Big Dream occupies, such as an address somewhere in the world, or it could represent the virtual space you create. Explain your space in terms of how it feels and what it looks like.

Take a shot at writing out your overarching vision. Make sure it includes someone doing something somewhere. Identify your tribe, cause, and space.

Overarching Vision: What's my Big Dream?

_____

_____

_____

_____

Now add your Purpose, Unifying Strategies, and Scorecard for Significance.

Purpose: What's the defining statement of my work?

_____

_____

_____

_____

Unifying Strategies: What's necessary for me to achieve this?

_____

_____

_____

_____

Scorecard for Significance: How do I know I'm hitting my target?

_____

_____

_____

Many of us are visual learners, and it's time for us to see an example of an OPUS and a CORE Six Pack. There are more examples online and in the appendix, but for now, here's mine.

Remember, I've "rinsed" this about a dozen times.[17] I've found that the more clarity I achieve, the more confidence I have. My builder, Chet, pushed me and helped me gain this clarity. Likewise, on your journey I encourage you to author yours within community. None of us were meant to do it alone.

If you don't have such a community, you'll find one waiting for you and your potential at DeeperPathBook.com We'd love to help you.

Kary's OPUS

A master in the art of living draws no sharp distinction between his work and his play; his labor and his leisure; his mind and his body; his education and his recreation. He hardly knows which is which. He simply pursues his vision of excellence through whatever he is doing, and leaves others to determine whether he is working or playing.

To himself, he always appears to be doing both.

L. P. Jacks

Overarching Vision: My Big Dream

Imagine a tribe engaged and on fire. A tribe that knows their identity, their purpose, and their context—who they are, why they are here, and where they should invest their lives. A tribe that believes the same things, but thinks different thoughts.

Imagine a cause built around authoring your OPUS and redeeming the day. A cause committed to belief, exploration, growth, and creation. A cause that pleases the Designer because it takes ownership of personal and holistic stewardship.

Imagine a space hardwired for lifelong learning. A space where authenticity breeds and truth in love flourishes. A space that regularly injects doses of acute Pain in order to overcome chronic Pain and create Souls on Fire.

Imagine a tribe, a cause, a space.

Welcome to my Big Dream—I've been waiting for you.

Purpose

The defining statement of my work: Connecting people to a process that ignites their souls on fire.

Unifying Strategies

What's necessary for me to achieve this?

- Personal Growth—By consciously adding value to myself I subconsciously add value to others; I can only export what I already possess.
- Synergistic Partnerships—By connecting and collaborating with a select few on the mutual journey, together we improve and accomplish more than we ever could alone.
- Transformational Experiences—By becoming more believable and by believing in others I'm qualified to create spaces that invite and challenge others to become Souls on Fire.
- Compelling Resources—By POPping my OPUS I'm able to provide content that catalyzes others to question, unmask, explore, overcome, and embody The Deeper Path.
- Compounding Influence—By strategically utilizing communication and sincerely investing in relationships my impact will go Deeper, reach further, and last longer.

Scorecard for Significance

How do I know I'm hitting my target?

PERSONAL GROWTH

- Words (Content)—Investing time in consuming and digesting content that challenges my paradigms.
- Actions (Experiences)—Engaging in experiences (that harmonize with my CORE) even though they might be uncomfortable, unfamiliar, or uncharted.
- Thoughts (Relationships)—Learning from teachers, mentors, and coaches who stretch my thinking because of their own commitment to personal growth.

Synergistic Partnerships

- Tribe—Building a tribe committed to building themselves and authoring their OPUS.
- Cause—Identifying entry points for people to consider and commit to the cause.
- Space—Designing locations (virtual and physical) that enable transformation to take place.

Transformational Experiences

- Teaching—Providing learning streams conducive for people to consider new information and ideas.
- Mentoring—Sharing experiences (both successes and setbacks) that help others see their own situations with more clarity.
- Coaching—Choosing to invest in a few high performers in a space, defined by open-ended questions that make them go Deep inside for the answers.

Compelling Resources

- Written (Think)—Writing authentically and passionately in a manner that invites others to question, unmask, explore, overcome, and embody The Deeper Path.
- Spoken (Hear)—Speaking truth to audiences that influences and engages their heads, hearts, and hands.
- Visual (See)—Creating mediums that visually connect viewers to captivating and contemplative content.

Compounding Influence

- Digital—Contributing content packaged in a way that connects with culture.
- Conversational—Embodying an understanding that communication is a dialogue that morphs and adapts as people do.
- Communal—Building a team Deeply committed to my Big Dream.

Kary's CORE Six Pack

1. WORLDVIEW—WHAT I BELIEVE

- God—I believe God, the Grand Overall Designer, is knowable and desires a relationship with every one of us.
- Humanity—I believe every human is created by God and in his image, and therefore possesses intrinsic value.
- Family—I believe family is the context in which we impart and embody our values and worldview.
- Life—I believe our life can be invested in a partnership with the divine in order to bring renewal and restoration to the world.
- Faith—I believe our faith keeps us grounded and centered in an unstable world.
- Truth—I believe truth exists and must be communicated and embodied.
- Work—I believe we each have a choice to approach work as either our labor or our OPUS.
- Abundance—I believe in abundance, in giving without receiving and pouring out grace and mercy on others.
- Pain—I believe potential always exists on the other side of Pain.
- Influence—I believe we need to gain influence with others before we try to lead them.
- Discipline—I believe excellence requires extreme discipline, focus, and effort.
- Time—I believe time is a limited commodity and should not be spent or wasted, but rather redeemed.

2. IDENTITY—WHO I AM

- Igniter—I am a new creation in and through Jesus Christ—free from fear and hypocrisy.
- Husband—I am committed to love and serve my wife, Kelly, unconditionally, growing closer to her as we grow older together.
- Father—I am father to three wonderful kids who need to see an example just as much as hear one.

- Friend—I am a loyal friend to a few, a friend who desires to be remembered as one who helped them in their times of need.
- Author—I am a writer who lets my readers peek into my process of working out my own questions about leadership, faith, and transformation.
- Coach—I coach a few high performers using a model of open-ended questions that increases their awareness, confidence, and belief in themselves.
- Speaker—I am a communicator who connects with my audiences and puts my whole heart into researching and relaying the truth in love.
- Achiever—I have a great deal of stamina and I take Deep satisfaction in being busy and productive.[18]
- Intellection—I am introspective and characterized by my intellectual activity.
- Futuristic—I am inspired by what could be and I inspire others with my visions of the future.
- Strategic—I am able to spot relevant patterns and create alternative ways to proceed.
- Ideation—I am fascinated by ideas and I easily find connections between seemingly disparate phenomena.

3. Principles—What I Value

- Specialization—I value developing and focusing on strengths.
- Exploration—I value venturing into new spaces, thoughts, and ideas.
- Communication—I value delivering information clearly and effectively.
- Participation—I value involving others.
- Preparation—I value investing the time and effort needed for excellence.
- Creation—I value original and authentic invention.
- Innovation—I value intelligent design.
- Perspiration—I value working hard.
- Validation—I value affirming others for their contributions.

- Recreation—I value having fun in what I do.
- Recommendation—I value feedback in order to grow and improve.
- Contemplation—I value reflection and introspection.

4. Passion—What I Love

- Ownership—I love leaving victimhood and taking responsibility for what I can control.
- Workmanship—I love making my life my greatest work.
- Stewardship—I love taking my gifts and talents seriously by investing in them.
- Craftsmanship—I love personal growth.
- Discipleship—I love discovering and applying what it means to follow Jesus more closely.
- Followership—I love learning from others.
- Leadership—I love adding value to others and influencing them to become better.
- Sportsmanship—I love interfacing with teams that push themselves to reach higher levels.
- Partnership—I love aligning myself with people who believe the same things but think different thoughts.
- Showmanship—I love people who love what they do and aren't afraid to show it.
- Championship—I love achieving goals.
- Marksmanship—I love accuracy and follow-through.

5. Purpose—Why I Live and Work

- Recognize—I help others become more self-aware.
- Maximize—I help others create the necessary momentum to start the journey.
- Minimize—I help others remove the noise that clutters their lives.
- Legitimize—I help others see the value of slowing down to reflect and write.
- Organize—I help others create the needed space to author their OPUS.
- Customize—I help others author their OPUS.

- Categorize—I help others identify their signature strengths.
- Synthesize—I help others make strategic connections that close their gaps.
- Prioritize—I help others do the first things first.
- Catalyze—I help propel others forward so they can achieve their dreams.
- Exercise—I help others develop a strong CORE.
- Optimize—I help others get the best return on their lives by holding them accountable to embody their OPUS.

6. Process—How I Will Do It

This is the detail that I author each month, initially within a coaching relationship and then eventually by myself. Remember, self-discipline is the ability to give yourself a command and obey it. Most of us initially lack self-discipline, but a good coaching relationship brings the necessary accountability. If you need help finding a good coach, just let me know. I'd love to help.[19]

Below is only an outline of my POP. I fill in the details each month and hold myself accountable to the baby steps of my Big Dream, my Overarching Vision. It might look like a rigid process at first glance, but it's much more fluid and organic once I get into my month. My perspective is to start with structure and clarity—because life will happen and we then need to flex and adjust. However, if we start with a fuzzy structure, then when life hits we'll never achieve our goals because we don't know what they are.

My January POP (Playbook of Productive Action)

Personal Growth

- Words (Content)—
- Actions (Experiences)—
- Thoughts (Relationships)—

Synergistic Partnerships

- Tribe—
- Cause—
- Space—

Transformational Experiences

- Teaching—
- Mentoring—
- Coaching—

Compelling Resources

- Written (Think)—
- Spoken (Hear)—
- Visual (See)—

Compounding Influence

- Digital—
- Conversational—
- Communal—

And that's just one month. I have eleven more to go. It might take a little work, but living the dream is worth it.

How did it feel going into your Scary Room? I trust it was exhilarating. This whole process takes time, but with each "rinse" we get more clarity. And each time we enter this room we get more courageous.

Authoring your OPUS and clarifying your CORE Six Pack allows you to discover your "Why." And just as importantly, it helps you see a way to live out your "Why." The process requires time, energy, and community, but those who take The Deeper Path emerge as Souls on Fire. And people on fire are the ones who change the world.

15

Five-Minute Sketch

Courage is fear with wings.

Audrey Moralez

Just like Captain Sully, we never know when life will call our number and demand a decision from us. We need to be ready for the moment and do the work ahead of time. When we prepare for the moment, the moment is prepared for us. And we are a world in desperate need of prepared people.

Captain Sully daily invested in himself, and life revealed he was the only pilot who could have landed the plane that infamous day. As we add value to ourselves, we make ourselves more valuable.

True masters of their craft realize the power of preparedness and the importance of process. A story about one of the greatest and most influential artists of the twentieth century, Spanish legend Pablo Picasso, adds some color to this truth.

Picasso was sitting at a table outside a Paris cafe. A woman came up to him and asked him to draw a portrait of her on a napkin. He complied, doodling as only he could. After he handed the sketch to her, she was pleased with the likeness and asked how much she owed him. Picasso requested the French equivalent of five thousand dollars. Aghast, the woman said, "But it only took you five minutes!" Smiling, the artist replied, "No, Madam, it took me my whole life."[1]

Picasso isn't the only artist in the room. Each of us has the opportunity to embody our OPUS every single day of our lives. Our masterpiece isn't some compartmentalized canvas but rather every square inch of our self.

And one day we will each give an account to The Artist on what we did with what we had.

Every takeoff has a landing.
And every book an ending.
This one is no exception.

Part of my Overarching Vision is watching my coaching clients find their voices and discover their own melody lines. Recently one of them, Audrey Moralez, shared a few notes from her song with me via email.

> The defining moment is not the glory moment. It is the glorifying moment. It's the gut-check moment. The moment that we decide to look up, show up, and man up. The moment when we decide that God's vision is farther-reaching than our own and we choose to trust His perspective. When fear takes flight and we begin to soar into our potential. Our defining moment is the moment we need to be courageous. And remember, courage is fear with wings.

By now, I'm writing this book with both hands. Funny how Pain slows us down in the beginning. This is why so many people never choose their Pain but ignore it instead.

As the weeks wear on, my shoulder is getting stronger and I'm letting my hurts heal me. Those incisions from the surgeon hurt initially, but they're just scars now, only reminders of the past.

In no time I'll once again be out on the course playing disc golf and in the living room wrestling with my kids. But to experience this potential, I had to first pursue my Pain.

And if you have any room to doubt, let me tell you, the Pain my physical therapists Eric and Nick bring with them has convinced me that PT stands for Pain and Torture. In all seriousness, though, I'm grateful to them because they made me better and stronger.

And so I challenge you to do this thing—afraid.

It's been said that if we put an adult brain inside a baby's body, it would take us until age eighty-three before we'd learn how to walk. We'd be so full of fear, self-judgment, blame, self-limiting beliefs, and shame that we'd spend eight decades stuck in an emotional and psychological self-sabotaging cycle.

Remember, stuck stinks! To reach higher ground, we must take The Deeper Path.

I leave you with one courageous thought.

Jump—and build your wings on the way down.[2]

Appendix A

Discussion Points

These questions, a few for each chapter, are meant to take you even Deeper.

Feel free to answer them on your own—or even better yet within your community or ours.[1]

Beneath the Surface

1. Do you know your "Why?" If so, what is it?
2. If not, what fears do you have as you begin this process?
3. Share about the last "Deep" person you met and the last "Deep" conversation you had.

The Deeper Path

1. What are three ways you try to mask your Pain?
2. What price would you have to pay if you went Deeper into your Pain and your potential?
3. Are you willing to pay it? Why or why not?

Chapter 1: A Routine Takeoff

1. Describe one of your "defining moments."
2. Were you prepared for it? Why or why not?

3. Do you feel prepared for your next "defining moment"? (Note: what it is isn't nearly as important as who you are.)

Chapter 2: The Melody Line

1. Describe the time when you felt most connected to yourself and to others.
2. In one sentence, describe how you want to be remembered.
3. Are you sitting in the Shire or are you on the journey, taking the ring? Explain how you know.

Chapter 3: The Door of Pain

1. What lies are you telling yourself that are keeping you stuck?
2. What's one area of life where you are practicing insanity (such as doing the same thing, but expecting different results)?
3. Explain a time when Pain caused you to reach more of your potential.

Chapter 4: Leaving the Nursery

1. How is comfort insulating you from your potential?
2. What are some coping strategies you use to be heard, to control life, to punish yourself or others, or to feel?
3. What are some situations in your life that can be defined as "good" Pain and "bad" Pain?

Chapter 5: The Little Difference

1. Which of the seven clichés (on pages 61–62) have you believed the most?
2. How have those beliefs held you back from your potential?
3. Take some time to refine your cross and your crown. How much clarity do you have?

Chapter 6: Step One: Question Your Condition

1. In what area of your life do you feel stuck?
2. What's your response to being stuck?
3. What's one area of your life where you are consciously competent?

Chapter 7: Step Two: Unmask Your Painkillers

1. Name a person who believes in you, and describe the relevant details.
2. How important is noise in your life? What's the price you have to pay to allow it in your life?
3. Write your own psalm expressing how you really feel about life.

Chapter 8: Step Three: Explore Your Wounds

1. What do you really want out of your life?
2. Now identify how you argue for what you *don't* want.
3. How do you self-sabotage your potential?

Chapter 9: Step Four: Overcome Your Excuses

1. What are your top three self-limiting beliefs?
2. Do you take inventory of why you *can't* do things?
3. What are some things you can't do, but wish you could?

Chapter 10: Step Five: Embody Your Healing

1. What's one thing you fear changing?
2. What do you fear failing at?
3. What area of your life do you fear succeeding in?

Chapter 11: One Happy Reunion

1. What's one area of your life where you've unwisely delegated away your responsibility?
2. If you died today, what would you regret not doing?
3. In light of your answer to question 2, is the Pain of regret stronger than the Pain of risk?

Chapter 12: God of Edges

1. Describe your relationship with God.
2. Are you content with the quality of it? Why or why not?
3. What unanswered questions do you have for God?

Chapter 13: Soul on Fire

1. Is your soul on fire? Why or why not?

2. If anything were possible, what would you ask for?
3. What's a decision you've been avoiding? Why?

Chapter 14: Author Your OPUS

1. What's your dream?
2. Does your life reflect labor or OPUS?
3. Reread the quote by L. P. Jacks. What word or phrase is most significant to you and why?

Chapter 15: Five-Minute Sketch

1. How will your life be different after reading *The Deeper Path*? Whom do you know who needs to read *The Deeper Path*?
2. Will you take the next step, get ever more clarity, and join a Deeper Path cohort?
3. What will it cost you if you don't take action?

Appendix B

Examples of OPUS

I've included two additional examples of OPUS here and there are many more online at DeeperPathBook.com. I believe seeing these will help you as you author yours. Both contributors are my coachees (coaching clients), and both examples are used with their permission.

The first example is from Linda Outka, a woman who loves resolving conflict. She founded Breakthrough Solutions after experiencing The Deeper Path Cohort. The second one is from Tim Walk (www. TimWalk.com), a twentysomething youth pastor who founded Interchange after experiencing The Deeper Path Cohort. I believe you will be encouraged by their clarity.

Linda's OPUS

A master in the art of living draws no sharp distinction between his work and his play; his labor and his leisure; his mind and his body; his education and his recreation. He hardly knows which is which. He simply pursues his vision of excellence through whatever he is doing, and leaves others to determine whether he is working or playing.

To himself, he always appears to be doing both.

L. P. Jacks

Overarching Vision: My Big Dream

Imagine a space where people feel it's safe to be real. Where people find common ground and new perspective when they are in conflict with one another. Where people explore new insights in places they feel stuck and discover breakthrough solutions that open doors to their potential.

Purpose

What's the defining statement of my work?

- Creating space where people feel it's safe to be real and discover breakthrough solutions.

Unifying Strategies

What's necessary for me to achieve this?

- Personal Growth—By regularly feeding my mind and spirit as well as connecting with mentors on a regular basis, I will give from the overflow of my internal reservoir and increase the value I add to others.
- Intentional Marketing—By being in strategic places on a regular basis to network, by offering complimentary services to individuals and groups, and by implementing other marketing strategies, I will add value to people's lives and cultivate relationships that will lead to coaching and speaking engagements.
- Breakthrough Solutions—Through coaching, speaking, and training, I will create space that allows people the freedom to experience transformation and discover breakthrough solutions. By designing programs that fit my passions and meet needs in others, I will add value to people and work from my strength zone.

Scorecard for Significance

How do I know I'm hitting my target?

Personal Growth

- Reading—Read books, articles, and blogs at least fifteen minutes a day.
- Reflection and Prayer—Pray and reflect at least a half hour each day.
- Coaching—Receive coaching twice a month.
- Mentoring—Initiate conversations and relationships with people who can mentor me in both my weaknesses and my areas of strength and for whom I can add value in return.

Intentional Marketing

- Public Places—Make new friends and reconnect with old acquaintances by being available in public places. (Add two names a week to my list of potential clients.)
- Chamber/Music/Church Events—Attend at least one event each month to add value to others and connect with potential coaching participants.
- Networking Groups—Become a member of a networking group and attend monthly meetings.
- Complimentary Coaching Sessions—Contact new people and old acquaintances to offer a complimentary coaching session (one session a week).
- Lunch and Learns—Offer free "Lunch and Learns" to pastoral groups, community groups, and businesses (one event a month).
- Writing—Publish articles, blogs, and books.

Breakthrough Solutions

- Coaching—Individual life coaching, business coaching, group coaching, premarital coaching, couples coaching, conflict resolution coaching, EQ-i debriefs/coaching.
- Speaking—Keynote business addresses, retreats, and conferences for pastors and staff.
- Training—Team building, conflict resolution training, MBTI team building, FIRO Element B team training, and workshops on corporate values and self-awareness.

Tim's OPUS

A master in the art of living draws no sharp distinction between his work and his play; his labor and his leisure; his mind and his body; his education and his recreation. He hardly knows which is which. He simply pursues his vision of excellence through whatever he is doing, and leaves others to determine whether he is working or playing.

To himself, he always appears to be doing both.

L. P. Jacks

Overarching Vision: My Big Dream

- To invite people to think differently through various mediums of story. Our interchange of ideas will leave each other with the ability to see the world differently.
- To initiate individuals and tribes into a lifelong process of growing, learning, and improving through consulting, coaching, and mentoring.
- To introduce resources that facilitate educational experiences and empower people with the love and power of God. These resources will propel people to discover who they are and to assist them in unleashing their potential.
- To ignite a generation to embrace the will and the Word of the Lord by personally introducing young people to Jesus Christ.

Purpose

What's the defining statement of my work?

- Propelling people to their next level through the interchange of ideas.

Unifying Strategies

What's necessary for me to achieve this?

- Personal Growth—Invest in my own growth as a leader through resources, partnerships, and experiences.

- Worship—Insist the presence of God take precedence in every area of my life.
- Concentric Relationships—Involve myself and add value to others personally, professionally, and spiritually.

Scorecard for Significance

How do I know I'm hitting my target?

PERSONAL GROWTH

- Be Sharp—Read regularly by reading leadership blogs, the Bible, and a devotional daily, and a book on ministry, spirituality, or leadership monthly.
- Be Coachable—Meet monthly with a mentor, someone I have a professional relationship with, where I can communicate my frustrations, share my dreams, and help shape my future. This mentor must be both competent and caring.
- Be Competent—Continue my education with Global University, averaging eight credits per quarter.
- Be Engaged—Go to two conferences a year, one to inspire me (fill my heart) and another to move my ministry (fill my mind).

WORSHIP

- Stay Fresh—Weekly take a Sabbath, a day devoted to spending time with those I love: God, family, and friends. The only agenda is fellowship.
- Stay Open—Consistently create vents in my life and ministry that will allow the Spirit of God to move freely in any service I lead, any decision I make, and any resource I prepare.

CONCENTRIC RELATIONSHIPS

- Be Available—Meet bimonthly with ministries I believe in. Meet biweekly with people whose destiny I have bought into and help them reach their dreams. Weekly mentor those who want to be in the youth industry.

- Be Creative—Interchange ideas through my blog weekly. Innovate products that will add value to youth and youth workers. Inspire students and those who work with students using the power of story. Interact with students from my tribe and provoke them to change.
- Be Generous—Introduce myself, my resources, and my prestige to those involved in the youth industry I can add value to, even though they may not necessarily add value to me.

Acknowledgments

Thanks to the entire team that helped me dig and find The Deeper Path.

Jesus—a powerful liberator. You keep me free.

Kelly—a sincere soul mate. You keep me strong.

Keegan, Isabel, and Addison—gifts from heaven. You keep me flexible.

David Branderhorst—an irreplaceable encourager. You keep me going.

Mike Myers—a kindred soul. You keep me sane.

Mom and Dad—an amazing pair. You keep me grounded.

Chet Scott—an inspiring builder. You keep me believing.

Angela Scheff—a brilliant mind. You keep me floating.

Josh Franer—an ingenious director. You keep me amazed.

Kathy Helmers—a persistent agent. You keep me creating.

Scott Fay—a generous believer. You keep me expanding.

Jamie Roiland—a detailed assistant. You keep me sharp.

Baker Books—a competent publisher. You keep me communicating.

Grace Church—a supportive church. You keep me thankful.

The John Maxwell Team—a vibrant community. You keep lifting my lid.

Your Secret Name Team—a Tribe on Fire. You keep me Ignited.

The Deeper Path Team—an incredible force. You keep enriching the message.

A special recognition to the very first trailblazers who joined The Deeper Path Team. You hold a special place in my heart: David Branderhorst, Linda Outka, Tim Walk, Elias Kanaris, Pam Pippin, Mike Clevenger, Chris Thompson, Jim Gernetzke, Daniel Evans, Jim Watters, Tamika Hodges, Heidi Hartmann, Desiree Arney, Bob Claxton, Mike Harbour, Nathan Eckel, Terry Wood, Kelly Heisler, Barbara Littles.

Notes

The Deeper Path

1. Thanks to Simon Sinek for his simple but brilliant model (the Golden Circle). "TED talk, How Great Leaders Inspire Action," YouTube video, 19:00, posted by TEDtalksDirector on May 4, 2010, https://www.youtube.com/watch?v=qp0HIF3SfI4.

Chapter 1 A Routine Takeoff

1. Chesley Sullenberger, *Highest Duty* (New York: HarperCollins, 2009).
2. "US Airways Flight 1549 Initial Report" (press release), *US Airways*, January 15, 2009.
3. Jeremy Olshan and Ikumulisa Livingston, "Quiet Air Hero is Captain America," *New York Post*, January 17, 2009.
4. Katie Couric, "Capt. Sully Worried About Airline Industry," *CBS News*, June 12, 2009, http://www.cbsnews.com/2100-18563_162-4791429.html, accessed July 22, 2012.
5. The greatest loss of life directly linked to a bird strike was on October 4, 1960, when Eastern Air Lines Flight 375, a Lockheed L-188 Electra flying from Boston, flew through a flock of common starlings during takeoff, damaging all four engines. The plane crashed into Boston harbor shortly thereafter, with sixty-two fatalities out of seventy-two passengers. Subsequently, minimum bird ingestion standards for jet engines were developed by the FAA.

Chapter 2 The Melody Line

1. "Melody," *Wikipedia*, http://en.wikipedia.org/wiki/Melody, accessed January 10, 2011.
2. "About One," *One*, http://www.one.org/c/us/about/3782/, accessed January 10, 2011.
3. Jeffery Cohn and Jay Moran, Why Are We Bad at Picking Good Leaders? (San Francisco: Jossey Bass, 2011), 97.

4. The American Academy of Pediatrics, "Children, Adolescents, and Advertising," http://pediatrics.aappublications.org/content/118/6/2563.full#ref-2, accessed July 22, 2012. See also E. Goodman, "Ads pollute most everything in sight," *Albuquerque Journal*, June 27, 1999.

5. John Maxwell, "People Will Summarize Your Life in One Sentence: Pick It Now," *Success*, http://www.success.com/articles/699-people-will-summarize-your-life-in-one-sentence, accessed July 27, 2012.

6. *Inception*, directed by Christopher Nolan (Warner Bros., 2010), DVD.

7. "M. Scott Peck quotes," *Thinkexist.com*, http://thinkexist.com/quotation/until_you_value_yourself-you_won-t_value_your/202530.html, accessed July 27, 2012.

8. Blaise Pascal, *Pensées and Other Writings* (Oxford: Oxford University Press, 1995), 10.

9. *The Fellowship of the Ring*, directed by Peter Jackson (2001; New Line Cinema, 2002), DVD.

10. www.BuiltToLead.com.

11. Henry S. Haskins, *Meditations in Wall Street* (New York: William Morrow & Co., 1940).

Chapter 4 Leaving the Nursery

1. "Endorphin," *Dictionary.com*, http://dictionary.reference.com/browse/endorphin, accessed March 18, 2011.

2. See Osuch, Noll, and Putnam, *Psychiatry* 62 (Winter 99): 334–45; Zlotnick et al, *Comprehensive Psychiatry* 37 (1): 12–16; and http://www.selfinjury.org/indexnet.html, accessed July 26, 2012.

3. "The Toxic Terabyte," *IBM Global Technology Services*, July 2006, http://www.935.ibm.com/services/no/cio/leverage/levinfo_wp_gts_thetoxic.pdf.

4. "First Knight Script—Dialogue Transcript," *Drew's Script-O-Rama*, http://www.script-o-rama.com/movie_scripts/f/first-knight-script-transcript-gere.html, accessed July 26, 2012.

5. "Acute vs. Chronic Pain," *Cleveland Clinic*, http://my.clevelandclinic.org/services/pain_management/hic_acute_vs_chronic_pain.aspx, accessed January 29, 2011.

6. Ibid.

7. "Back Pain and Statistics," *American Chiropractic Association*, http://www.acatoday.org/level2_css.cfm?T1ID=13&T2ID=68.

8. Ibid.

9. "Core Strength Training For Reducing Back Problems & Injuries," Sports Fitness Advisor, http://www.sport-fitness-advisor.com/core-strength-training.html, accessed January 29, 2011.

10. "Shadowlands Script—Dialogue Transcript," *Drew's Script-O-Rama*, http://www.script-o-rama.com/movie_scripts/s/shadowlands-script-transcript-winger-hopkins.html, accessed July 26, 2012.

Chapter 5 The Little Difference

1. Sam Parker and Mac Anderson, *212° The Extra Degree*, (Dallas: Word, 2005), 1–2.

2. Ibid, 19.

3. Christopher Sign, "Surveillance videos capture image of Giffords being shot from three feet away," January 18, 2011, http://www.abc15.com/dpp/news/region_central_southern_az/tucson/report:-surveillance-videos-capture-images-of-giffords-being-shot-from-three-feet-away#ixzz1kDZUcW6e.

4. "Gabrielle Giffords Shot: Congresswoman Shot In Arizona," *The Huffington Post*, January 8, 2011, http://www.huffingtonpost.com/2011/01/08/gabrielle-giffords-shot-c_n_806211.html.

5. Mark Kelly, *Gabby: A Story of Courage and Hope* (New York: Simon and Schuster, 2011), 1.

6. "Gabby Giffords: Finding Words Through Song," *ABC News*, November 14, 2011, http://abcnews.go.com/Health/w_MindBodyNews/gabby-giffords-finding-voice-music-therapy/story?id=14903987#.Tx6PaZihCFI.

7. Katie Moisse, Bob Woodruff, James Hill, and Lana Zak, "Gabby Giffords: Finding Voice through Music Therapy," http://abcnews.go.com/Health/w_MindBodyNews/gabby-giffords-finding-voice-music-therapy/story?id=14903987, accessed July 26, 2012.

8. Dan Nowicki, "Gabrielle Giffords' political future still unclear," *USA Today*, January 8, 2012, http://www.usatoday.com/news/nation/story/2012-01-08/giffords-political-future/52453566/1.

9. Amy Bingham, "Rep. Gabrielle Giffords to Step Down from Congress," *The Note*, January 22, 2012, http://abcnews.go.com/blogs/politics/2012/01/rep-gabrielle-giffords-to-step-down-from-congress/.

10. Ibid.

11. Ibid.

12. Ibid.

13. "Passion," *Dictionary.com*, http://dictionary.reference.com/browse/passion.

14. "Passion," *Merriam-Webster.com*, http://www.merriam-webster.com/dictionary/passion.

15. Max De Pree, *Leadership Is an Art* (New York: Dell, 1989), 11.

Chapter 6 Step One

1. "The Matrix (1999)," *Philosophical Films*, http://www.philfilms.utm.edu/1/matrix.htm, accessed July 26, 2012.

2. "The Matrix," *Wikiquote*, http://en.wikiquote.org/wiki/The_Matrix, accessed July 26, 2012.

3. "Memorable quotes for The Matrix," *IMDb*, http://www.imdb.com/title/tt0133093/quotes, accessed July 26, 2012.

4. "70 Million Americans Feel Held Back by Their Past," *Barna Group*, November 3, 2011, http://www.barna.org/culture-articles/532-70-million-americans-feel-held-back-by-their-past.

5. "Anaïs Nin," *Wikiquote*, http://en.wikiquote.org/wiki/Anaïs_Nin, accessed July 26, 2012.

6. "Saint Augustine Quotes," *Quotes.net*, http://www.quotes.net/quote/42932, accessed July 26, 2012.

Chapter 7 Step Two

1. "The Poetry of Emily Dickinson: Reader's Guide—Other Works/Adaptations," *National Endowment for the Arts*, http://www.neabigread.org/books/dickinson/readers05.php, accessed July 26, 2012.

2. Pascal, *Pensées*.

3. "Talk: Thomas Edison," *Wikiquote*, http://en.wikiquote.org/wiki/Talk:Thomas_Edison, accessed July 26, 2012.

4. "Steve Jobs' 2005 Stanford Commencement Address: 'Your Time Is Limited, So Don't Waste It Living Someone Else's Life,'" *Huff Post*, http://www.huffingtonpost.com/2011/10/05/steve-jobs-stanford-commencement-address_n_997301.html, accessed July 26, 2012.

5. Michka Assayas, *Bono* (London: Penguin, 2006), 253.
6. John W. James, Russell Friedman, *The Grief Recovery Handbook* (New York: Harper Collins, 1998), 48.
7. See Psalms 7, 26, 35, 52, 55, 58, 59, 69, 109, 137, and 139.
8. "Imprecatory Psalms," *Theopedia*, http://www.theopedia.com/Imprecatory_ Psalms, accessed July 26, 2012.
9. *The Lion King*, directed by Roger Allers and Rob Minkoff (1994; Walt Disney Pictures, 2011), DVD.

Chapter 8 Step Three

1. Julie Corliss, "Bridge the intention-behavior gap to lose weight and keep it off," *Harvard Health Publications*, March 10, 2011, http://www.health.harvard.edu/ blog/bridge-the-intention-behavior-gap-to-lose-weight-and-keep-it-off-201103101729.
2. "Memorable quotes for The Matrix," *IMDb*, http://www.imdb.com/title/ tt0133093/quotes, accessed July 26, 2012.
3. God's first command over humanity was to "be fruitful; govern the earth and rule over it" (see Gen. 1:28).

Chapter 9 Step Four

1. Bruce Lowitt, "Bannister stuns world with 4-minute mile," *Saint Petersburg Times Online Sports*, http://www.sptimes.com/News/121799/news_pf/Sports/Bannister _stuns_world.shtml, accessed July 26, 2012.
2. Ibid.

Chapter 10 Step Five

1. "Simon Cowell Net Worth," *Celebrity Net Worth*, http://www.celebritynet-worth.com/richest-celebrities/actors/simon-cowell-net-worth/ accessed June 13, 2012.
2. John C. Maxwell, *The Difference Maker* (Nashville: Thomas Nelson, 2006), 138.
3. Eric Hoffer, *Ordeal of Change* (Cutchogue, NY: Buccaneer Books, 1976).
4. "Biography for Anatole France," *IMDb*, http://www.imdb.com/name/ nm0289787/bio, accessed July 27, 2012.
5. John C. Maxwell, *The 21 Irrefutable Laws of Leadership* (Nashville: Thomas Nelson, 1997).
6. "Charles DuBois quotes," *Searchquotes.com*, http://www.searchquotes.com/quo tation/The_important_thing_is_this%3A_To_be_able_at_any_moment_to_sacrifice _what_we_are_for_what_we_could_bec/301242/, accessed July 27, 2012.
7. Hoffer, *Ordeal of Change*.
8. Rick Warren, Twitter post, January 8, 2011, 2:32 p.m., https://twitter.com/ RickWarren/status/23869616900018176, accessed July 27, 2012.
9. "John Henry Newman Quotes," *BrainyQuote*, http://www.brainyquote.com/ quotes/quotes/j/johnhenryn107044.html, accessed July 27, 2012.
10. Theodore Roosevelt, "Citizenship in a Republic," Speech at the Sorbonne, Paris, April 23, 1910, *Theodore Roosevelt Association*, http://www.theodoreroosevelt.org/ life/quotes.htm, accessed July 27, 2012.
11. Brad Lomenick, Twitter post, April 19, 2011, 9:15 a.m., https://twitter.com/ bradlomenick/status/60376054606467072, accessed July 27, 2012.
12. Marianne Williamson, *Return to Love* (New York: Harper Collins, 1992), 190–91.
13. Viktor E. Frankl, *Search Quotes*, http://www.searchquotes.com/quotation/ Fear_may_come_true_that_which_one_is_afraid_of./68749/, accessed July 27, 2012.

Chapter 11 One Happy Reunion

1. "Hudson Flight 1549 HD Animation with audio for US Airways Water Landing," YouTube video, 2:08, posted by airboyd on March 2, 2009, http://www.youtube.com/watch?v=jZPvVwvX_Nc, accessed July 27, 2012.

2. Robert Kolker, "'My Aircraft': Why Sully may be the last of his kind," *New York Magazine*, February 1, 2009, http://nymag.com/news/features/53788/.

3. Katie Couric, "Capt. Sully Worried About Airline Industry," CBS News, June 12, 2009, http://www.cbsnews.com/2100-18563_162-4791429.html, accessed July 22, 2012.

4. "Viktor E. Frankl Quotes," Good Reads, http://www.goodreads.com/author/quotes/2782.Viktor_E_Frankl, accessed July 27, 2012.

5. "Flight 1549: An Emotional Reunion," CBS News, July 6, 2009, http://www.cbsnews.com/2100-18560_162-4783594.html, accessed July 27, 2012.

6. "LOST Ending Scene," YouTube video, 4:21, posted by Oilime87 on May 24, 2010, http://www.youtube.com/watch?v=e3D6EG35WP0.

7. Todd Henry, *The Accidental Creative* (New York: Portfolio Hardcover, 2011), 216–17.

8. Catechism of the Catholic Church, Article 294, http://www.vatican.va/archive/ENG0015/__P19.HTM.

9. *Serendipity*, directed by Peter Chelsom (2001; Miramax Films, 2002), DVD.

10. Steve Jobs, "'You've got to find what you love' Jobs says," *Stanford Report*, June 14, 2005, http://news.stanford.edu/news/2005/june15/jobs-061505.html, accessed August 14, 2012.

11. Viktor Frankl, *Man's Search for Meaning* (Boston: Beacon Press, 1959), 93.

Chapter 12 God of Edges

1. C. S. Lewis, *Mere Christianity*, (San Francisco: HarperSanFrancisco, 1952), 137.

2. "The Confessions of St. Augustine Bishop of Hippo," *Cyber Library*, http://www.leaderu.com/cyber/books/augconfessions/bk1.html, accessed July 27, 2012.

3. *Shadowlands*, directed by Richard Attenborough (1993; Warner Bros., 1999), DVD.

Chapter 13 Soul on Fire

1. This thought inspired by a conversation with Michael Hyatt. Thanks, Mike!

2. "Friedrich Nietzsche quotes," *Thinkexist.com*, http://thinkexist.com/quotation/he_who_has_why_to_live_can_bear_almost_any/186996.html, accessed July 27, 2012.

3. Dan Ariely, *Predictably Irrational* (New York: HarperCollins, 2008).

Chapter 14 Author Your OPUS

1. For more information, visit www.BuiltToLead.com.

2. L. P. Jacks, *Education through Recreation* (New York: Harper & Brothers, 1932), 1.

3. Kenneth A. Tucker, "A Passion for Work," *Gallup Business Journal*, http://gmj.gallup.com/content/379/passion-work.aspx, accessed June 13, 2012.

4. "Gallup Study Indicates Actively Disengaged Workers Cost U.S. Hundreds of Billions Each Year," *Gallup Business Journal*, http://gmj.gallup.com/content/466/gallup-study-indicates-actively-disengaged-workers-cost-us-hundreds.aspx, accessed June 13, 2012.

5. Kicking a dog is sad enough in and of itself.

6. Thanks for this now-universal metaphor go to Jim Collins, *Good to Great* (New York: Harper, 2001).

7. John C. Maxwell, Twitter post, April 18, 2011, 5:00 a.m., https://twitter.com/JohnCMaxwell/status/59949439560851456, accessed July 27, 2012.
8. Albert Camus, http://bornofanatombomb.tumblr.com/post/2156188098/from-return-to-tipasa-1952, accessed July 27, 2012.
9. Henry David Thoreau, *Wikiquote*, http://en.wikiquote.org/wiki/Henry_David_Thoreau, accessed July 27, 2012.
10. Oliver Wendell Holmes, "The Voiceless," *Eldritch Press*, http://www.eldritch press.org/owh/vless.html, accessed July 27, 2012.
11. "Alice in Wonderland Quotes," *Lenny's Alice in Wonderland site*, http://www.alice-in-wonderland.net/books/alice-in-wonderland-quotes.html, accessed July 27, 2012.
12. Discover more in the appendices or at www.DeeperPathBook.com.
13. "Back Pain and Statistics," *American Chiropractic Association*.
14. "Core Strength Training For Reducing Back Problems & Injuries," *Sports Fitness Advisor*.
15. Visit www.DeeperPathBook.com for examples and worksheets.
16. Seth Godin, *Tribes: We Need You To Lead Us* (New York: Penguin, 2008), 1.
17. *Rinsing* is a term we use to describe editing.
18. These next five were identified and defined with help from Tom Rath, *Strengths-Finder 2.0* (New York: Gallup Press, 2007).
19. Just visit www.karyoberbrunner.com/coach.

Chapter 15 Five-Minute Sketch

1. Leda Karabela, "No, Madam, It Took Me My Whole Life," *Why Hesitate*, August 7, 2011, http://yhesitate.com/2011/08/07/no-madam-it-took-me-my-whole-life/, accessed July 27, 2012.
2. This line inspired by science fiction author Ray Bradbury. See Lev Grossman, "R.I.P. Ray Bradbury: He Jumped Off Cliffs and Never Hit the Ground," *Time Magazine*, http://entertainment.time.com/2012/06/06/r-i-p-ray-bradbury-he-jumped-off-cliffs-and-never-hit-the-ground/#ixzz1zgRmkPxh, accessed July 27, 2012.

Discussion Points

1. Visit our community at www.DeeperPathBook.com.

Kary Oberbrunner has a burning passion—igniting souls. Through his writing, speaking, and coaching, he helps individuals and organizations clarify who they are, why they are here, and where they should invest their time and energy.

Kary struggled finding his own distinct voice and passion. As a young man, he suffered from severe stuttering, depression, and self-injury. Today a transformed man, Kary invests his time helping others achieve their true potential. He is the founder of Redeem the Day, which serves the business community, and Igniting Souls, which serves the non-profit community.

The author of several books, Kary also serves as a founding partner on the John Maxwell Team. He and his wife, Kelly, are blessed with three amazing children. Connect at www.KaryOberbrunner.com.

TAKE YOUR NEXT STEP

Join a Deeper Path Coaching Cohort

Imagine author Kary Oberbrunner or one of his Certified Coaches leading you through a transformational process where you journey through your Pain and into your potential.

Imagine finding clarity by authoring your OPUS and strengthening your CORE.

Hundreds of people have found freedom and purpose through this powerful experience. Participants can join from anywhere in the world.

FIND OUT MORE AT DEEPERPATHBOOK.COM

What's the cost of not living in light of your true potential?

BRING KARY INTO YOUR BUSINESS OR ORGANIZATION

IGNITER. AUTHOR. COACH. TRAINER. SPEAKER.

_____

Kary knows the importance of choosing the correct speaker. The right one sets the stage for success, and the wrong one for disaster. Kary's authentic approach, combined with superb content, positions him as a top choice for many businesses and nonprofits. He customizes each message and training to achieve and exceed the objectives of his clients.

CONTACT KARY TODAY TO BEGIN THE CONVERSATION
KaryOberbrunner.com

The Deeper Path Team
Certified Speakers, Trainers, and Coaches

WE CAN'T CHANGE THE WORLD ALONE.

WE NEED A TEAM.

We call it a tribe of Souls on Fire.

If you're looking to join a team that helps people process

through their Pain, realize their true potential, and discover

their Why, consider joining The Deeper Path Team.

Do what you love and get paid for it. How cool is that?

If our team fits your OPUS, then we'd love to chat with you.

There's a spot waiting for you in our lineup.

Join us at
THE DEEPER PATH
Live Event

Imagine The Deeper Path live and in 3D. We all learn differently, and studies show that an experience engaging the senses allows the message to sink in deeper.

INVEST IN DISCOVERING YOUR WAY BY FIRST DISCOVERING YOUR WHY.